JOHN WHITE GEARY

JOHN WHITE GEARY

During the Civil War

JOHN WHITE GEARY

Soldier-Statesman

1819–1873

By

HARRY MARLIN TINKCOM

UNIVERSITY OF PENNSYLVANIA PRESS

PHILADELPHIA

1940

FOREWORD

THIS volume initiates a significant publication program—a series entitled *PENNSYLVANIA LIVES,* which is designed to do honor in brief, readable biographies to the men and women of Pennsylvania in many fields of activity who shared in the history and development of the state, but whose contributions have hitherto been overlooked.

It is fitting to have the series open with the biography of a man whose life span coincided with one of the most stirring periods of American history, a man who participated in many important national events, culminating his active career as governor of his native state—a Pennsylvanian, in short, who made history.

John White Geary was a member of an American profession now extinct. He and his professional brethren were to be found on the far-flung American frontier supervising and directing the adjustment of institutions created in older communities to fit the needs of the new. These state-builders wrote many thrilling pages in the annals of the "furious 'forties" and "fateful 'fifties," for their labors were heroic, tragic, even comic. Geary and his fellows had to deal with the vagaries of conduct not usually found in such profusion in the regions whence they came. They met every sort from resourceful statesmen and sober citizens to bandits and the sorriest charlatans, and to succeed in these outposts under construction the directors had to possess unusual persistence, ability, versatility, and luck.

General Geary gravitated to successive centers of the unusually dynamic activities of these years. In the Mexican War, in California, in Kansas, in the Civil War, and finally in the gubernatorial chair of post-war Pennsylvania, he could count few months in which the ordinary pursuits of a peaceful and quiet life were ever known to him. Upon these pages is spread a colorful story which is in reality more than a biography, for it is an illustration of a vital phase of the enterprise so typical of the creative years in the history of the Republic.

ROY F. NICHOLS

University of Pennsylvania
May 1940

CONTENTS

I

EARLY LIFE

In following the activities of John White Geary we must survey the most exciting and trying events of the United States's roaring and turbulent nineteenth century. Where the fighting was thickest, where the stakes highest, there we find our central figure. He was attracted to conflict and action as is a moth to flame.

Our country emerged from the formative crucible inured to attacks from enemies at home and abroad. The birth of the Republic was attended by solemn and dangerous circumstances, but no less dangerous, no less precarious were the critical events which accompanied its early youth. The Republic, a babe in a world of avaricious neighbors, plagued by serious internal disorders, grew in strength and stature only with the aid of strong and unselfish men. Among them Geary, statesman and warrior, is a fine example.

John White Geary was born on December 30, 1819, near the peaceful little town of Mount Pleasant, in Westmoreland County, Pennsylvania. His father, Richard Geary, a native of Franklin County, and a descendant of that hardy pioneer stock, the Ulstermen, was a man of liberal education and refinement. He married Margaret White, a resident of Washington County, Maryland. Shortly after their marriage the couple moved to Westmoreland County, in western Pennsylvania, where Richard planned to establish himself in the iron industry, a business which was risky and highly competitive. He operated the Mary Ann Furnace, and although he labored strenuously, his enterprise could not be placed on a paying basis. Eventually he was forced to withdraw from his project and turn over everything to his creditors, losing his entire original investment. This failure left him in straitened circumstances with many outstanding bills yet to be paid.

He now relied upon his education and opened a school. He taught Westmoreland County children for the rest of his life, but then, as now, teaching was far from being a lucrative profession. In spite of a sincere effort to recuperate his finances, he died insolvent, leaving the members of his family dependent upon themselves for support.

Although never affluent after the collapse of his business, Richard Geary continually strove to give his boys a substantial amount of education. He had four sons in all, but the first and third unfortunately died before reaching maturity. The second son, Edward R. Geary, taking full advantage of the learning his father had so thoughtfully provided, studied for the ministry, and in due time became an eminent Presbyterian clergyman. Early in his life he moved to the state of Oregon, where he became an influential figure in the development of that region. The youngest son, John White Geary, was enrolled at the time of his father's death as a student at Jefferson (now Washington and Jefferson College), Canonsburg, Pennsylvania. Feeling it incumbent upon him to help provide for his mother, he opened a school of his own at the early age of fifteen. Hard work and thrift eventually enabled him to return to Jefferson College, from which he was graduated.

With his college course behind him he looked about for a means of livelihood. His experience as a teacher had convinced him that that profession was not adapted to his taste, so in a search for opportunity he went to Pittsburgh, where he obtained a position as clerk in a wholesale house. This too proved unsatisfactory, and after a while, yielding to a natural partiality for mathematics, he began the study of civil engineering. After mastering the principles of that vocation his thirst for knowledge was not yet satisfied. Feeling that a thorough comprehension of law would prove an invaluable aid to his chances for a successful career, he took up that study and was eventually admitted to the bar. At this time, however, he fully intended to adopt engineering as his life work. This insatiable desire for knowledge had now thoroughly grounded Geary for his later public services.

Both of the specialized courses he had taken after leaving Jefferson College proved extremely worth while.

Intent now upon utilizing his studies in engineering, he sought and secured a position in Kentucky, where he worked for the State and the Green River Railroad Company in making a survey of several public works projects. With the remuneration obtained from these engagements and from a successful land speculation, he was now able to return home and place in his mother's hands all the money necessary to satisfy the claims of his deceased father's creditors. This had always been his aim, and now that it was accomplished he felt greatly relieved.

Once again in Pennsylvania, Geary was not long in finding lucrative employment. He secured a position with the Allegheny Portage Railroad Company, and in a very short time he was promoted to the rank of Assistant Superintendent and Engineer. This railway was a unit in the chain of transportation links between Philadelphia and Pittsburgh, one section in the three hundred and ninety-five-mile span of canals and railroads which had been constructed by the State in response to the demand of eastern merchants that a more rapid means of transportation be created to connect the port of Philadelphia with the Ohio. It was hoped that this line of transportation would restore much of Pennsylvania's commerce with the West and meet the competition of the Erie Canal which was opened in 1825. The trip from the coast to Pittsburgh was beset with many difficulties, the greatest of which were the Alleghenies. To meet the challenge of this mountainous region a group of daring engineers built the famous Allegheny Portage Railroad. It extended over the rugged country between Hollidaysburg and Johnstown, a distance of thirty-six miles. In order to send coaches up and down the mountain the engineers devised a series of ten inclined planes, five on either side. Stationary engines, located at the top of each plane, raised or lowered the cars by means of strong cables. The relatively level spaces between each plane were traversed either by horse or engine power. As the double-tracked railway stretched westward to Johnstown it passed through what was probably the first railroad tunnel in the United States. Built in 1832 it pierced a spur in the mountain nine hundred and one feet in length.

This extraordinary undertaking was one of the world's most unique railway experiments, and so revolutionary was the project that many European engineers came to inspect it. It was one of the finest examples of empire building in America. Even Charles Dickens, who traveled over the railroad on his American tour, was mildly impressed.

But as the great American passion for speed continued to assert itself the Portage Railroad was found to be too slow. In 1857 it was sold to the newly organized Pennsylvania Railroad Company, which had already built a continuous line of rails across the Alleghenies. The old inclined planes were left to rust and rot themselves into limbo, their picturesque attraction supplanted by the Horseshoe Curve, then as now the scenic climax on a journey by rail from Pittsburgh to Philadelphia.

Today a monument stands on the William Penn Highway, near the town of Cresson, commemorating the remarkable achievements of those heroic pioneers in the field of locomotion. And if one is so inclined he may wander off the beaten path to travel again the old Portage trail, where little that is physical remains except the old stone sleepers that bore the rails, grass-grown and forgotten.

II

THE MEXICAN WAR

For some time trouble had been brewing between the United States and Mexico over the Texas Territory. The annexation of Texas had been a bitter issue in Congress. Because of the intense desire of southern congressional members to secure additional slave states, and the determination of certain northern members to prevent such action, the ensuing quarrel presaged the gigantic conflict between the states which was soon to come. Aided by a fairly strong expansionist sentiment which prevailed in the country, it was not long before those favoring the admission of Texas succeeded. The House of Representatives on February 25, and the Senate on March 1, 1845, passed resolutions which made Texas a member of the Union. Tyler signed the resolution on March 1, three days before Polk was inaugurated. Polk had been so interested in the measure that he had hurried to Washington to force it through.

Of course Mexico had never recognized the independence of Texas, and now that the United States had taken her into the fold, little friendliness existed between the two countries. The immediate cause of the rupture between them concerned the boundaries. The United States claimed the Rio Grande as her proper frontier, while the Mexicans insisted that our claims did not extend beyond the Nueces River. It was to be expected that Polk would back up the expansionist claim, having been elected to the Presidency on that platform. Now in the chief seat of government, he forthwith prepared to satisfy the American demand by sending General Zachary Taylor into the disputed territory with a small force. Obviously, the President wanted the quarrel to be resolved one way or another: either the Mexicans would tolerate American soldiers in the contested area and accept the situation with as much grace as possible, or else they would attempt to drive Taylor from his position by violence. Mexico, now forced to make a decision, sent General Arista

5

into the territory. He came into conflict with the troops of General Taylor in April 1846, and in the following month President Polk informed Congress that war existed with Mexico.

Now that we were engaged in war, the President asked for ten million dollars and fifty thousand men. This summons for volunteers succeeded in obtaining enough recruits to more than subdue Mexico. The call flew rapidly to Pennsylvania and circulated among the towering Alleghenies to fall upon the ready ears of John White Geary. The young engineer hesitated not a moment in responding to the demand for soldiers. He would gladly help Polk "conquer a peace."

With an eye to the future, Geary had always tried to prepare himself for life and the unexpected events which might come. This was previously evidenced in his desire to train himself in the fields of law and engineering. The art of warfare was no exception. For some time he had been intensely interested in military history and tactics. In addition to studying the technique of arms in an academic fashion Geary had been vigorously promoting schemes which would help perfect the volunteer system. A keen interest enabled him to rise quickly from the rank of a private to that of brigadier general. The brigade, composed of members from Cambria and Somerset counties, elected him to this rank.

To show their appreciation of Geary's services and abilities, the brigade members selected him as a delegate to the National Military Convention, held at Washington, D.C., December 10, 1842. He represented the Twelfth Military Division of the Pennsylvania Militia.

The time and energy spent in improving the volunteer system had served Geary in good stead. With the knowledge gained through his military efforts he was better prepared to be of aid in the war which was now at hand. Among the first to volunteer, he enrolled on December 18, 1846, quickly organized a company which he appropriately named the "American Highlanders," and set off from the Cresson Summit for Pittsburgh. Through the early pioneer towns of Ebensburg, Armagh, and Blairsville the little troop marched at a rapid rate of speed to arrive in Pittsburgh on January 3, 1847. The town presented a wild and riotous scene in those stirring days. They were welcomed enthusiastically by the citizens, and were later bidden a hearty farewell with just as much vigor when they left for the distant fields of action. Their stay was brief but hectic, marked by numerous carousals and free-for-all fights as they elected officers to command them.

The Highlanders joined the Second Pennsylvania Regiment under the command of Colonel W. B. Roberts, and on January 6 Geary was elected lieutenant colonel by a vote of 591 to 373 over his nearest competitor, William Murray.

The Second Pennsylvania was not long in the gala city. Haste was imperative, for Santa Anna, the Mexican commander, was proclaiming with vivid oaths the fearful havoc he would create among the invaders from the North. So on January 9 the regiment, amid great excitement and rejoicing, departed for far-off Mexico, the theatre of war. With flags and martial music in the air the militant band chugged down the rolling Ohio to Cincinnati. Here an unstable boat failed to operate, and a two days' suspension of travel was necessary to make the steamer riverworthy once more.

After the balky craft had been repaired, the warriors continued their voyage to New Orleans, which was reached on January 18. They were held in the city for several days by heavy rains, but when the weather cleared they took passage on a vessel bound for Tampico.

The student who wishes to follow the progress of doughty young Geary through our war with Mexico finds his path eased and his task made thoroughly enjoyable by a diary kept by the far-faring soldier himself. Beginning his entries on December 31, 1846, the wintry day which found him leading the Highlanders away from Cresson Summit on the road to war, he faithfully chronicled his adventures until the conflict ended. Through adversity and triumph, battle and calm, sickness and health, he continued to cover the pages of his little notebook with his personal experiences and observations. The diminutive volume survived the heat, rains, and battles of Mexico; and now, after the lapse of almost a century, it enables us to live again with Geary, the soldier and the man. As an invaluable document, both human as well as historical, it deserves generous space in these pages.

The entries covering the Lieutenant Colonel's trip from Cresson Summit to New Orleans are quite brief, and it is not until the troops have embarked at New Orleans on January 24, 1847, that he has time to take fuller notes. Let us turn to that day then, and follow our diarist.

Jany 24. Tremenduous rain. Quite a deluge—2 feet of water in camp ground—Men wade out. Baggage all wet—Camp broken up—embarked on board the ships. "I.N. Cooper"—Genl. Veazie, and Ocean. Companies B.D. and G embarked on board the Veazie under my command—Companies C.F and K on the Ocean under Maj Brindle, the rest on the Cooper under command of Colonel Roberts.

Jany 25th. Rain.—26th Rain—doing nothing.—The soldiers of the Mississippi Regt. dying in great numbers.

Jany 27th. Clear and fine. Men and officers employed drying clothes.—fight between a Miss. Volunteer and a Pennsylvanian.

Jany 28th. Tremenduous storm, which prevented our starting to Mexico.

Jany 29. Left New Orleans, arrived at the mouth of the S.W. pass—country between, level and uninteresting, being principally prairie.

Jany 30th. Lay waiting the arrival of the I.N. Cooper 24 hours. Within 3 miles of the Bar. Light house on Starboard, and Pilot town on Larboard. This town consists of 15 or 20 houses, meanly built on blocks or piles.—This day we saw several porpoises, and some very large fish.

Jany 31. Sunday.—The day on which sailors delight in going to sea. We passed over the bar, towed by the Steamer Tennessean. The day was perfectly calm and the Gulf smooth as Glass. and during the whole day we only drifted 12 miles from the shore. As we passed the bar I ascended the rigging and asked three cheers of the battalion for the glory, honor and prosperity of our native country, which was heartily responded to.—At night nought was visible to the eye save the light house at the bar. "It seemed like a star in lifes tremulous ocean." So sweetly described, in the song I have so rapturously listened to—so sweetly sung from the mellifluous lips of my beloved wife.[1] 10 o'clock at night, appearances indicate a storm.—As the shores of my beloved native land recede from my view my feelings were indiscribable.—Our course S.W. by W. (I forgot to mention that the Missippi regt. and our own occupying 6 ships, and about twenty others were in sight of each other.) 11 o'clock— The scene from the quarter deck is one of the most interesting & contrasts strongly with the scene within the ship where nought is heard but the loud curses of the soldiers, while the fair face of the heavens and the Gulf have neither sound, cloud or ripple.

Feby 1. I arose this morning—head giddy, stomach sick, ate but little breakfast.—The ship rocks considerably, a large number sick.—10 o'clock, a government steamer passed us, with a large number of passengers on board—bound for New Orleans. Capt Fairfield of the vessel quite accommodating.—Our officers agreeable—Soldiers orderly and easily managed scarcely requiring a guard—"Genl. Veazie" ahead.—"I.N. Cooper" behind about 9 miles.—Immense numbers of porpoises make their appearance, and many small fish are about the vessel, the soldiers try to angle them but they cant come it.—The day is hazy and very pleasant. Ship becalmed, about 40 miles from South Pass Light house. Nought to be seen of land on any side. 12 o'clock. Latitude 26° 30'. Long[.]90° from Greenwich. Storm commences blowing. I get very sick—also a great number of men. Storm rages at night.—

Feby 2. Storm continues with unabated fury, and increases at night. Men nearly all sick[.] I remain very sick.—and consequently unable to write—

Feby 3rd. Storm abated about 10 o'clock, the weather cleared up pleasant but cool—I am recovering, and so are the soldiers[.] I this day saw numerous "Nautila" or little "*sailors*". they are very beautiful. We are now sailing S.W. the direct course for Tampico and are about 270 miles from the Balize, fine N.E. breeze.—Sun sets clear—nothing interesting this day.—The Physicians on board the "Veazie["] are Dr. Fletcher & Grimshaw

Feby 4th. Day pleasant, fine breeze.—Saw a large number of porpoises in the ev[en]ing. My health is better, the officers &

[1] In 1843 Geary had married Miss Margaret Ann Logan, of Westmoreland County.

soldiers are generally improving in condition[.] We are now 275 miles from Tampico. We expect to arrive there on Sunday next. God willing

Feby 5th. Nothing new to-day the same monotous scene presents itself to view.—Not a ship has made its appearance, for the last 48 hours.—Capt. Fairfield is a gentleman of the kindest deportment.—The crew of the ship very orderly.—The water upon which we sail appears as blue as indigo—We are drifting northward, and hope for fairer winds[.] I am tired of the sea, and would prefer being among rolling logs than to have my home on the rolling waves.—

Feb. 6th. "Once more upon the deck I stand", and nothing but the same dreary watery waste presents itself to my view. The wind is still fair and until it changes we cannot reach Tampico. At 10 o'clock a sloop makes her appearance bound for New Orleans. Nothing else happens during the day, but a perfect calm, which leaves us like a perfect log on the Ocean.

I spend part of my time reading my Bible & my tactics, part of it looking into the deep blue waves, and part of it I amuse myself watching the various modes of cookery among the soldiers. Some of them are dirty, but most of them are clean and live as well as the officers in the Cabins.—They often wish themselves in their mother's pantries to get a "skin full" of the good things of this life.

Feby. 7th. This morning we found ourselves within 8 or 10 miles of the Mexican Shore, in about 15 fathoms of water, perfectly becalmed—and the water green as grass. The enemy's shore appears inhospitable and rugged, the trees and bushes being covered with vines and thick clusters, which I suppose to be what the Mexicans call chapparel. in order to prevent our drifting ashore the ship cast anchor. At 12 o'clock we raised anchor and set sail—course S.E.—being about 30 miles north of the mouth of the river Santander. Along the coast there lies a Lagoon (Lake) which skirts the whole western coast of the Gulf and if it were not for a few cross bars intervening, it would be navigable for small craft.—Every preparation is made on board to prevent surprise from the enemy who doubtlessly at this time are watching our motions. we are now about 150 miles from Tampico[.] This is Sunday—the day of rest. How cruelly it is used under the licenses of war.—Oh! that I could visit one of our Pa[.] churches for an hour or two. . . . and talk about matters and things in general and then return.—But when this war is over, we all will know how to appreciate the good things of life. The society of beloved friends, and the benefits of a Christian Country.

For the next eight days the *General Veazie* experienced intermittent periods of calm and storm. On February 10 a terrific gale battered the little ship about with such fury that the Lieutenant Colonel was sure that "nothing less than an almighty hand could have sustained us and preserved us from the destruction of a watery grave." Three days after the storm subsided a soldier by the name of Fred[erick] Shriver was found to have smallpox. Great excitement prevailed. This was the beginning of an epidemic which caused the companies under Geary's command no little trouble, and later delayed their departure for Vera Cruz.

After cruising rather aimlessly about the shore for a few days the island of Lobos was sighted by Geary on February 18. It was on this small island that General Scott concentrated his troops before the attack on Vera Cruz.

Feby 18. With a fair wind last night and this morning we arrived within sight of Lobos by 10 o'clock and reached our anchorage at 12 M. After dinner Capt Fairfield and myself (in the Captain's "Gig") came on shore.

I never was more agreeably disappointed on reaching a place in my life—instead of finding a burning sandy and arid Island as I had anticipated I found it a very pleasant place.

It is situated on a coral rock surrounded with shoal water and a reef distant from the shore from 100 to 300 yards. The island is about 2½ miles in circumference and its surface about 15 or 20 feet above the level of the sea. It is thickly covered with orange, Lemon, Lime, Banian, Gum-Elastic and other trees, bearing fruit. . . .

The greatest abundance of fish are found in the shoal water around the Island—The red fish is the most abundant. they vary in length from 1 to 4 feet—and are of the most delicious flavor. —The shoal water affords a very fine place for sea bathing and is much enjoyed by the soldiers.

The island is infested with immense numbers of large rats and mice, supposed to have originally come here from the wrecks of vessels with which the coasts abound and of which no doubt many a melancholy tale might be told if some "Robison Crusoe" were only reserved to give us the reminisces. Vast numbers of striped lizards about 10 or 12 inches in length, run around like so many scared spirits, also square crabs of extraordinary fierceness.—these rats, lizards, & crabs I am assured by men whose veracity I have no reason to doubt made a regular attack upon the first soldiers who landed here and tried every means to prevent encroachments upon their sacred rights. Ants of every description & spiders abound on the island.

Water is obtained by digging 7 or 8 feet, but is so sweet and tasteless as to be faintish and disagreeable to the taste.—The climate is exceedingly mild, being favored with sea breezes from whatever quarter the wind blows. The shipping anchored south of the island is perfectly safe from the northers which are the most dangerous winds in this climate except squalls and tornadoes. (So much for the island of Lobos).

I found the "I.N. Cooper" & the "Ocean" at anchor—They arrived here on Monday last. the troops had disembarked and were in camp, generally in good health. One case of small pox occurred on the Ocean.—The troops on the "Veazie" are prevented from landing on account of Schriver's case.—Great excitement prevails in camp for fear of that dreadful disease and every precaution is being made to avoid contagion.

I remain in Camp over night & find the regiments here 1st & 2nd Pa Vols. South Carolina Vols. 1 regt from New York, and one from Louisiana—Quite an emulation prevails among the officers as to who shall assume the command of the Island. everything as yet is in confusion, each regiment being under the command of its Col. Genl. Scott & Genl. Worth are expected here in a few days. their arrival will eclipse the present satellites just as easy [as] the glorious orb of day puts out the lamps of night—The number of troops encamped on the Island is between 4 and 5.000.—with 500 regulars on ship board. This Island is said to have been one of the favorite retreats of that celebrated pirate Lafitte.—Tradition says much money is buried here.—The soldiers are busy searching— One Spanish dollar and some coppers is all that as yet has rewarded their labours.—Three Mexican prisoners have been taken here. they came here to sell oranges and other fruits.—Circumstances made it apparent that they were spies. they are under strict guard during the day and ironed at night.—

I consider this Island a perfect paradise, when taken in comparison with the Ship Veazie and our recent wanderings upon the Gulf.

Feby 18th. Slept last night in "quarantine" on the soft side of a plank. Weather fine and clear.—Decision of the Field Officers of the different regiments against the landing of the troops from the "Genl. Veazie."—Another meeting called to reconsider the same matter at 9 o'clock A.M. tomorrow.

Feby 20th. By special invitation I witnessed the manouvering of 210 men on board the War Ship St. Mary's drilling as though engaged in a naval conflict.—Nothing new occurred to-day.—I visited the Ship Veazie & found all hands doing well.—

Feby 21. Sunday. Heavy rain and high wind last night. The norther continues.—Four ships laden with troops arrived this morning. One of them carrying Maj Gen Scott.—The matter of precedence between Col Butler and Wyncoop was referred to Genl. Scott and he decided in favor [of] the latter. Consequently Wyncoop is commander of the island. The Missippi & the Louisiana Regiments received orders to leave Lobos and embark on board their transports for Tampico.—The Missippians lost 12 men on the passage from New Orleans to this place—One of the vessels bringing the Louisiana Volunteers was wrecked on Cape Roxo—the soldiers were all saved—but the Governments stores were all lost, and in order to prevent the ship from falling into the hands of the Mexicans it was burnt by the Americans.

Feby 22nd. Seven companies of our regt were drawn up in line to-day—for dress parade[.] they make a splendid appearance, and are a crack regt. The day was celebrated with much spirit by many of the volunteers.—12 vessels arrived to-day.

Feby 23.rd. I am Field Officer of the Day. Nothing strange occurs or worthy of note.—The New York regt is all here—Wrote to wife.

Feby 24th. Troops received orders to embark on transports forthwith—Sharp work on hands, probably, before many days.

Feby 25. The Louisiana and Mississippi Volunteers receive orders to embark and proceed to Tampico—which they do to-day—

Feby 26th. The first regt Pa Vols and the South Carolina Regt receive orders to embark on board their transports. The Pa regt embarks. A norther springs up and prevents the embarcation of the S.C. regt.—I pay a visit to Gen Scott. in the evening I take a sea bath. Thirteen vessels of different [*sic*] arrive in the harbor.

Feby 27th. Small pox increases rapidly on board the Gen Veazie. The troops continue to embark.

Feby 28th. Genls. Worth, Twiggs, & Smith arrive. Troops continue to arrive.

March 1. Seven Cos. of the 2nd Regt [Pennsylvania] embark. And concluded on the 2nd. The weather is fine.

Mar 3rd & 4. The troops on the Veazie & myself receive orders to remain and garrison Lobos until every vestige of small pox is eradicated from amongst us

Mar 5th. My three companies are encamped on the island in good spirits but much shattered in health.

6th, 7th. 8th. 9th 10th. I have had a very bad spell of the diarhoeah during these days & been unable to keep up my diary, and also unable to attend to any other duties whatever. Nothing very important has occurred. The departure of the fleet from this place for Antonio Lizardo was a very imposingly grand spectacle. Sixty two ships left upon time and thirty two more followed soon after—Here I could not refrain from tears. to behold myself and my devoted band thrown out of the army— (a despised and forlorn hope) deprived of the companionship of our friends in the army—and worse than all, to be deprived of joining in the glorious career of honor which appears in embryo before our gallant little army.

But, in every circumstance, it is consoling to think and to know, that God causes all things to work together for good and for his own purposes. I will therefore dry the lachrymose fount, and try to make the best of what is left. And it is possible that in Gods providence our stay on the Island of Lobos will be much for my good and that of my command. And that our course will yet be honorable and bright.

Thus, under the force of necessity, he stayed on the little patch of green that was Lobos, and heart-broken, surrounded by the dread smallpox, he thought that his trip of thousands of miles had resulted only in landing him almost within reach of his goal. Would he miss the goal itself, the actual campaign in Mexico? Although bitterly disappointed, he was stoically resigned to his fate and comforted by the thought that God had so willed it; all was for the best.

When General Scott ordered his troops to leave Lobos he was

planning to attack and capture the important city of Vera Cruz as soon as possible, for the terrible yellow fever season was about to descend on the coast, and he was afraid it would have a more devastating effect on his army than even shot and shell. Once the city was in his possession he could then take his men into the interior, away from the fever region.

Discarding direct assault on the city as being too dangerous, and starvation of its inhabitants a too lengthy process, he then selected siege and bombardment as the most logical method.

Orders were given to land the troops on March 8, but when the glass fell, indicating an approaching norther, the orders were countermanded. When the next day dawned clear and bright, Scott prepared to land ten thousand men off Sacrificios Island, just east of Vera Cruz. The landing was accomplished without a single mishap. No Mexicans had appeared to offer resistance.

During the next few days Scott arranged his men at the rear of the city in a half-circle several miles long. Now was the time for artillery, but hindered by a lack of transportation facilities, as well as a norther which lasted for four days, the work went forward slowly. It was not until March 22 that the guns were so placed as to do serious damage to the beleaguered town. On that day Scott threatened the city with bombardment and asked for its immediate surrender. After he had been answered with a refusal, the American batteries began firing in the late afternoon. The heavy fire raged all next day and night, but when Scott thought it was proving somewhat ineffective he asked Perry, the fleet commander, for naval guns big enough to crack the city walls. These were provided, and the damage they were able to do spread consternation and dismay in Vera Cruz. Many people cried for surrender, especially after the terrible cannonade of March 25, when, according to Cadmus M. Wilcox, in his *History of the Mexican War*, "the firing was increased to 180 shot and shell per hour."

Under this devastating hail of metal the morale of the city rapidly wilted. Negotiations for surrender began, and on March

27 terms of capitulation were agreed upon. Two days later Vera Cruz was occupied by the American troops. Scott now prepared to march into the interior of Mexico.

While the American army is battering Vera Cruz into submission, Geary cares for his troops on Lobos, reads his Bible, does considerable fishing, and writes frequently to his beloved wife back in Pennsylvania. He also derives a great deal of pleasure from writing to his infant son Edward.

Time is heavy on his hands, and the days imitate each other in dullness. On March 14 Geary listens to a heavy cannonading coming from the direction of Vera Cruz, and stirs with impatience at this life of inactivity which has been forced upon him. But on March 29 he reports hopefully that the smallpox patients are nearly all well, and the subject of leaving begins to occupy their attention. A few days later the patients arrive in the main camp, perfectly clean and well, and preparations are made for departure. On April 8 all the soldiers are put on board ship. During the night the Lieutenant Colonel sleeps soundly, but feels "fatigued by sleeping in a soft bed."

The *General Veazie* slowly ploughs its way through the Gulf of Mexico and reaches Vera Cruz three days after leaving Lobos. The day the ship reaches its destination Geary writes his first entry after reaching Mexican soil.

April 11th. With every stitch of canvas spread to the breeze we passed along at the rate of 4 miles per hour. At 10 o'clock A.M. we were hailed by a "Man of War" from whom we obtained information of the surrender of the City of Vera Cruz and the Castle St Juan De Ulloa [San Juan de Ulúa].[1]

About 3 o'clock P.M. we arrived at the far famed city.—After casting anchor, Capt Fairfield and myself went ashore. I reported to Gen. Scott the arrival of my detachment, and visited the city and its suburbs. And found that although the city presented a beautiful appearance, but upon nearer inspection found the whole of mean and contemptible in the extreme. —Every house being a fortress in itself, and not a single house

---

[1] This was a strong stone fort at Vera Cruz, which gave the victorious Americans surprisingly little trouble.

has glass in it, lattices being used instead thereof. The Castle is strong in the extreme, and 500 men (Americans I mean) would be able to defend it from the invasion any force whatever from without.—The custom house and palace in the city are good buildings, also several cathedrals, all of which are built in the old Gothic Stile of the most contemptible materials.—The whole city presents a scene of dilapidation.

April 12th. Landed my troops about ½ a mile below the city, and encamped and christened it Camp "Restoration"—I received two letters to-day from Mrs. Geary. feel very happy . . . Our camp is thickly covered with balls that were shot during the battle.—

The entries for the next four days are very brief. He records nothing new except the burial of a Captain Wilson of the Columbia Guards.

[*April*] *17th.* We left camp Restoration (or Washington) and proceeded 4 miles and encamped without tents in the sand upon the Beach of the Gulf.

April 18th. We started this morning in company with the Tennessee Cavalry, S.C.—Geo. & Alabama Regts Vols. under command of Gen Quitman,[1] and travelled about 15 miles and encamped on the bank of a beautiful creek.—We had a slight skirmish here, in which 2 of our men were wounded and 1 of the Mexicans.

The country through which we travelled is generally rolling and hilly—The ground sandy, without stones. The road good, but very dusty, which is very light and white and made every thing of the same color. . . . The Chaparel grows to the height of 16 or 20 feet—has leaves like Hemlock. is thickly covered with thorns like cow's horns—and presents the appearance of an old peach orchard. Every thing is mingled with Cactus of at least 6 or 7 different species, some of them at least 50 [feet?] in height—There are also some prairie covered with herds of

[1] From this time on until the fall of Mexico City Geary remained permanently attached to the brigade of General J. A. Quitman, the fiery Southerner who had previously served under Zachary Taylor. He had been sent to Vera Cruz by Taylor when that General had been requested to send part of his men to General Scott by order of President Polk. Taylor had roared at this apparent injustice. But a little later, and still roaring, he attacked the Mexicans at Buena Vista and chased them ingloriously from the field. Taylor's star was clearly on the ascendancy.

cattle, wild horses, asses, & mules.—Green corn & sweet potatoes
are abundant—Parrots and all kinds of birds with beautiful
plumage are abundant. Mexico is the land where flowers bloom
and birds sing.

I visited the Hacienda De Santa Anna called "Manjo de
Clavo", 2½ miles from camp.

April 19. Remained in camp waiting for the rear of our train.

April 20. Travelled about 18 miles and encamped at the
"Puente National"—And passed several other beautiful bridges
on the way—The pass at the national bridge is one of the strongest in Mexico. Yet it was left undefended and we are suffered to
pass by it and encamp by it unmolested.

On the day that Geary left the Gulf of Mexico (April 18,
1847), with the three companies of the Second Pennsylvania
Regiment that had been detained at Lobos, the American troops
under the command of Scott met and defeated an army led by
Santa Anna, who had fortified the hilly region around the village
of Cerro Gordo. The first American commander to encounter
the Mexicans in that section was Brigadier General D. E. Twiggs.

On April 8 Twiggs, with the second division of regulars,
started out for Jalapa, the first large town on the route from
Vera Cruz to the City of Mexico. He was in the van of all of
Scott's troops. Although he had been warned that a substantial
body of the enemy lay in front, Twiggs, on April 12, was marching boldly along in the region of Cerro Gordo when the Mexicans suddenly attacked in force. Santa Anna had laid an ambush
which almost proved fatal to the Americans. Luckily they were
able to retreat without serious loss.

While Twiggs was trying to decide what to do next, General
Scott arrived on the fourteenth. He immediately began to prepare plans for attack.

The bloody battle that ensued was a complete victory for the
American troops. Charging over a rugged terrain, so precipitous
and difficult that Santa Anna believed it would defy a rabbit,
the attackers completely demoralized the Mexicans and chased
them away in hopeless confusion. The mercurial Santa Anna
had failed again.

The Mexican casualties were estimated at over a thousand, while the American loss amounted to only thirty officers and 387 men, of whom sixty-four were killed. Eighty-five hundred Americans had faced from twelve to eighteen thousand of the enemy.

Geary describes the scene of conflict as he passes through:

April 21. Started at ½ past 4 o'clock and about 1 oclock arrived at the encampment at the foot of the *hill* (mountain I should say) called Sierra Gordo. here is a fine stream of water, which is crossed by a fine stone bridge. four miles from this place the battle of Sierra Gordo was fought on Sunday the 18th inst—There are about 200 wounded at this place.

April 22nd. Passed the Battle Ground. It is a very strong pass, and well fortified. Much stronger than the pass at the Puente National. About 500 cannon were taken and 10,000 stand of arms. Also 5.000 prisoners, among whom were Genl. Vega & Jeleah [?] & about 200 commissioned officers all of whom were set at liberty on parole of honor except the Generals. Morales a Mexican Genl. was killed. Genl. Shields of the Americans was wounded. The rout of the Mexicans was complete. They left between 300 & 400 dead on the field. All their ammunition, ordinance & all other stores. The road through which we passed was strewed with dead Mexicans, horses, caps, coats, waggons, accoutrements, etc. which the Mexicans had cast away in their haste to escape the fury of Col Harneys cavalry, who pursued them hotly.[1] Santa Anna barely escaped with his life, leaving behind him his carriage & $35.000 in money.—The stench arising from dead carcasses on the road was very annoying and in many instances almost suffocating.—

We encamped in view of one of Santa Anna's haciendas 8 miles from Jalapa.—

April 23. Arrived in Jalapa about 10 oclock A.M. and proceeded without stopping to the encampment of our regt. 3 miles west of the town.—Here I had the pleasure of meeting David Logan—When I arrived in camp I was greeted by my Regt. with three hearty cheers—[The major part of Geary's regiment had fought under Colonel Roberts at Cerro Gordo.]

[1] William S. Harney first distinguished himself while fighting against the Indians in Florida. So brilliantly did he perform at Cerro Gordo that he was raised from Colonel to Brevet Brigadier General.

April 24—We may probably be encamped here for 8 or 10 days and I shall have time to fill my notes and observations a little more fully. In the afternoon I visited Jalapa. it is decidedly the best town I have seen in Mexico. it contains about 6.000 inhabitants, who are of a much superior class to those in Vera Cruz. Jalapa is situated in the midst of a most fertile neighborhood at the foot of a lofty mountain, at an elevation of 4.000 feet above the sea. The neighborhood is noted for the medical article "Jalap" which takes its name from the city.—The climate here is one eternal spring and admits of but little change. Continual verdure clothes every species of vegetation.—The same trees are constantly in bloom, and yielding their ripe fruit and greens.

The lofty volcanic peak "Orizaba" is in sight of this place about 40 miles distant. It rears its head far above the clouds to the height of 17,370 feet—Several hundred feet is covered with perpetual snow, and emits smoke from its top.—The "Calzada" or paved road from Vera Cruz to this place is truly a beautiful affair. Many a beautiful bridge on the way. Consists of solid masonry thrown over wild and steep ravines.—The road consists of 11 paralel ranges of stone about 3 feet apart, and the vacancies between the ranges is neatly paved. The ditches on the sides of the road are very durable, and in many places are made of cement.

The citizens of Jalapa gave Santa Anna 40.000$ as an inducement for him not to make a stand in it.—There are a number of Yankees in this neighborhood engaged in manufactures tavernkeeping, etc.

April 25. I am "Officer of the Day" and will be engaged all the time.—Nothing happens worthy of Place.

April 26. We still remain in "Camp near Jalapa". The wet weather commences to-day, and the effect is terrible upon our soldiers, who sleep in bush huts.—

April 27. 28. 29. 30. Rains every afternoon about 3 oclock.— Health of the troops declining—diarrhoea prevails to a great extent—Several soldiers have died. . . .

May 1st. Wrote to Wife and to W. W. Logan, also to Edward.—

May 2nd. I am Officer of the day. A large amount of Mexican uniforms distributed among the soldiers—great fun among the boys.

May 3rd. The prospect of our departure for the City of Mexico begins to brighten.

May 4th. All Orders countermanded.—Maj Gen Patterson is ordered home.—The Alabama, Georgia, 3rd & 4th Illinois, & 3 regts. from Tennessee are ordered to New Orleans to be mustered out of the service. [Their terms of enlistment had expired.] The first & 2nd Pa. the New York, & South Carolina Regts are formed into a new Brigade under Gen Quitman.

May 5. The above named troops leave for their homes.—

May 6th. The Illinois troops leave for home. I take leave of David Logan—Our Regt. take up the line of March for Jalapa where we are placed as a part of the Garrison—We take up our quarters in Barracks far from being comfortable.—

May 7th. Frederick Daw of Co. B. dies and is buried in an appropriate manner. We arranged our quarters in pretty good stile, but have some difficulty about the modus operandi of our cooking establishments.—We have nothing very good to eat, but we have good health to digest a soldiers' fare—Upon examination of the city of Jalapa I find I have underrated its population at least 50 per cent—The city is very compactly built, and must contain about 12.000 inhabitants. No news from home since Feb 11th—I wrote to wife by Maj Genl. Patterson and a few days ago to W. W. Logan and wife—

Every house here is built like a fortress, and they are joined together in such manner as to form a wall around each square, with gaits as entrances for men and horses.

The women are not handsome, but some of them are comely. [Some] have the scientific flirt.

May 8. I am "Officio dela Guardio" to-day, and am on duty most of the day in order to make myself duly acquainted with city and its suburbs. . . .

May 9. Sunday—The Indians and Mexicans thronged the market "Plaza" to overflowing long before daylight, with at least ten times the amount of stuff usually brot in on other days. Every delicacy usually produced in a tropical and middle climate can here be obtained, though at very high prices.— Chickens, worth in the U.S. about 10c are sold here readily at 50c & turkeys at 1.00 and 1.50 according to size—and every other thing in about the same proportion. . . .

May 10th. Every thing "in statu quo" so far as regards the management of the place

I am amused at some of the customs and manners of the country—The women of the higher classes ride on the right side of the horse, equiped with splendid skirts and "sombreros" and very frequently bare headed—The lower classes ride on both sides of the horse "id est" straddle legs.—with a handkerchief pinned around their heads. I have not yet seen a single head dress of any description on a female in Mexico, except the *sombrero*.—The market women sit in the hot sun all day, vending their vegetables without any cover or shield whatever, with their unmentionables upon the bare ground.

May 11. 12. 13th. To a soldier in garrison every thing becomes common, and that spice of life *change* being lost, scarcely any event occurs worthy of being chronicled.

May 14th. This day is noted for the long looked for arrival of the *big train*—It consists of 500 waggons and about 500 pack-mules bringing provisions and ammunition for the Army. Also $500.000 in specie—that won't be hard to take when a man is out of money.—

May 15th. Went to the Bull Bait—Five bulls were fought and whipped—by nine men—one on horse back

May 16. 17. Nothing new has occurred. I am officer of the day on the 17th—

May 18. Drew my pay from the time I was mustered into service, 3 months and 26 days[.] $556.37—$500 in a Treasury note, $50 in gold, & 6^{37}/_{100}$ in silver.—

May 19th. This is a day noted for the public punishment of 4 thieves, 3 belonging to the U.S. Army and 1 to the 2nd Regt of Penna. Vols. . . . They each received upon his bear back, forty stripes, save one, with the *cat*,—their heads shaved, and were driven through the principal streets with the word robber (with letters 2 inches in length) placed upon their backs with the Rogue's March played after them.—Although these men doubtlessly deserved punishment, yet the mode in which it was inflicted is a relic of barbarism, and ought not to be continued in an enlightened age.

From May 20 to June 17 Geary continues his unexciting garrison duties at Jalapa. Nothing of any great importance occurs. However, on June 9, after attending a soldier's funeral, he reflects bitterly on the indifference of American philanthropy toward the needy troops in Mexico:

In this war we have lost very many brave men. Many now languish in sickness, and are almost destitute of proper medical attendance, of nourishing diet, of kindness. No one to speak kind words to alleviate their sufferings.—Our country is full of philanthropy. Every thing possible is there done for suffering foreigners. Men risk their lives to preach the gospel to the Chinese, they spend their fortunes for irish emancipation, to sustain the Irish peasantry in their starving condition. Ship loads after ship loads are sent gratuitously for their relief. But although the Army of the U.S. may suffer morally from want of preceptors. Its sick without proper treatment, food or attendance. The philanthropy of our country seems to be asleep, or to forget that gospel truth "that charity begins at home", or never think that they could alleviate the sufferings of the brave men who now languish in Mexico.—There never was a prettier field for the philanthropists of our country to display that kindness than those in question. A few religious instructors are essentially necessary to restrain the morals of our soldiery. Much good could be done by sending those things calculated for sick men, or affording those men the means to procure it for themselves, and also there should be plenty of good attendants for the sick. It may be objected that the government should do all this, true. But she does not. Neither can she in the extensive line of her business ever be expected to meet the exigencies of every case. philanthropy can always find sufficient to do in the train of an invading army.

On June 17, in accordance with instructions received the day before, Geary led nine companies of the garrison to an encampment three miles west of Jalapa. This was a preliminary movement in preparation for the march to the Castle of Perote, farther north.

June 18th. The remainder of the troops from Jalapa and the whole train consisting in about 400 waggons arrived in Camp, also Gen. Cadwallader [General George Cadwalader] to whom I surrender my command—fuss between Capt Kerr and Richard McMichael.

19. In accordance with orders issued last night, we are prepared to start to Perote. We travel about 10 miles.—I commanded a detachment of four Companies as a portion of the front guard. We [had] but little skirmishing but fatigued our men much by flanking and driving a small body of Mexicans before us. Nothing occurred during the day worthy of entry.

We encamped at the village of Lahoya [La Hoya] on a beautiful plain surrounded by immense peaks. I was officer of the day. We travelled over the most delightful and picturesque country in the world. The clearness of the atmosphere enabled us to see all the state of Vera Cruz—even to the Gulf. The breaking of the surf upon the coast though at the distance of sixty miles was perfectly visible.—The high barren peaks contrasted strongly with the beautiful vales between them.—At Lahoya we experienced a very cold night, and although I had my clothes all on, and two blankets I was nearly frozen. All the country bore evident marks of volcanic eruption and violent convulsions—

June 20. We started on our march this morning at 5 o'clock and immediately entered the celebrated pass of Lahoya which I consider is only second in strength to Cerro Gordo—Strong fortifications covered every hill on each side of the road which upon examination we found were unoccupied. they are all strong and if well defended would be hard to turn.[1] The road wound itself in a narrow valley over a deep bed of lava, which has been cast from the surrounding volcanoes, and across the valley at intervals of 200 or 300 yards were strong breastworks thrown up to be defended by cannon. but for 2½ miles we did not see a single Mexican. At last we discovered a few on an immense peak on the left of the road. A portion of the 1st Artillery was sent up to cut off their rear.—Co. "G" of my command was sent to reconoitre the face of the hill—and Co. "A" to deploy over a level space of woodland between the hill and the road, and Capt Caprous Co. of the 1st Arty. and the American Highlanders (Co B) & the Cambria Guards (Co D) were left under my command upon the road.

The Battle was opened by us with 4 shots of a 12 pounder under command of Col. Childs—after which the Mexicans showed themselves in vast numbers and came down the hill to cross the road in our front. As soon as they arrived in the road they were attacked by Capt Walhers mounted riflemen. And I was ordered to charge with my command—This Co's B & D did in the finest stile with the *grand yell* driving the Mexicans at a

[1] The fortifications Geary mentions had been abandoned by the Mexicans directly after their defeat at Cerro Gordo.

rapid rate through a field of barley over a bed of rough lava and through a dense chapparel, pushing them clear over the hill into a deep valley on the right. from the top of this hill I ordered a volley to be fired which drove the Mexicans far in our advance. I ordered the charge to be continued down the hill, at the foot of which I discovered a cave, into which I directed the men, which was found to be well stored with every luxury to eat, together with live turkeys & chickens, also blankets, trinkets, and jewelry all which was quickly plundered and the charge continued—We continued the charge 4 miles, keeping up a desultory fire all the time.

At last a halt was ordered and we were forced to obey and return to the road. We returned from the chase and after a long march found ourselves at the village of Las Vegas [Las Vigas].—During the fight we [met] a portion of the 1st Regt Pa Vols. who had come from Perote.—The whole country through which we passed was totally destroyed by fire as well as the sword. The Mexicans were variously estimated at about 1000 footmen and 200 cavalry.—Their loss was about 80 killed and six prisoners. Our loss—1 wounded.—At the point where we left the road "D" Company came under the command of Lieut Hyer. Capt Murray being too weak to follow. As we passed through Las Vegas about ¼ of it was on fire, and I understand that it was all burnt to ashes. We arrived in Camp having travelled 12 miles and fought the *battle of Lahoya,* before night. And our boys (that is B & D) had a splendid supper from the plunder of the enemy.

June 21. We started very early and marched in our usual order. We arrived at Perote at 12 oclock. pitch our camp under the Guns of the Castle. . . .

Geary stayed at Perote several days under the command of General Cadwalader, who had received orders to wait for General Pillow to arrive. When that General made his appearance, the troops were again put in motion for Puebla, the second city in importance to the Capital, with a population of about eighty thousand. Here they remained while Scott concentrated his small army for an attack on Mexico City itself.

Finding little of consequence to enclose in his notes, the Lieutenant Colonel amused himself, when not suffering with dysentery, by walking about to observe the town and its environs. But not at all pleased with the inclement weather and the inhabitants of Puebla, whom he considered the "most execrable" he had yet seen, he awaited impatiently the order to again move forward.

On July 29 Geary heard a humorous story which he gleefully wrote in his diary:

I cannot refrain from relating the following anecdote. Some time ago when Capt. Kearney with 26's of dragoons approached within 25 miles of the City of Mexico with a flag of truce, the news of his approach was magnified by the time it reached the city into the approach of our whole army. The Mexicans being much alarmed and having a full lake of water, let it out in hopes of stopping us by immersing us to the knees in water. But we were not there, and the city being somewhat lower than the surrounding country, was flooded, much to the annoyance of the citizens to the depth of almost 4 feet with water. Heavy rains set in at the same time, and they have up to the present time, been in a pretty predicament.

While waiting for the arrival of General Franklin Pierce, who was on his way up from the coast, the troops at Puebla continued their training and, having become more accustomed to the climate, were in fairly good condition. Many, however, still remained on the sick list.

Finally, on August 6, General Pierce arrived with 2,500 men, and orders were received to get ready for the march to Mexico City. The lethargic camp sprang to life, and all was bustle and hurry. Puebla was left behind on the eighth, and during the next four days they marched thirty-six miles. This brought them to the top of the mountain, 10,500 feet above sea level, where they could look down into the valley of Mexico. Once in the valley the little army would have a difficult time retreating. But very few thought of retreat, forward was the word. On August 11, 1847, they went down into the valley, faced by tremendous hardships and obstacles. J. F. H. Claiborne, a biographer of Quitman, sums up the situation as follows:

When the American General Scott, with only 10,000 men, a large proportion of them new levies that had never seen fire, and but imperfectly drilled, left Vera Cruz, Jalapa, and Puebla, with 80,000 inhabitants and 100,000 rancheros and guerrillas in his rear, and plunged into the heart of a great empire to attack its capital, occupied by 180,000 people, defended by 35,000 soldiers, and environed by formidable fortifications bristling with cannon served by skillful artillerists, he found no precedent for so daring a movement in military history.

On August 18 Geary arrived at the village of San Augustin, about ten miles south of Mexico City. Here much skirmishing occurred on the front and sides. In fact, as the army threatened the capital, it attacked and in turn was attacked from almost every angle. In two days it fought the battles of Churubusco, San Antonio, and Contreras. Scott described all these battles as one, labeling them collectively the Battle of Mexico.

Santa Anna, the ubiquitous Mexican commander-in-chief, tried without success to drive back the invaders who, in an amazingly short time, were in position to attack the city itself.

While all this fighting was in progress, Quitman had been ordered to take the Second Pennsylvania Volunteers and a detachment of veteran United States marines to protect the important depot at San Augustin, where were located the siege, supply, and baggage trains. Quitman, with an eye to fighting and glory, asked to be relieved, but his application met with no success. Geary, too, chafed under this inactivity when all around him guns were roaring and the flag was going forward. On August 20 they were ordered to advance, but when halfway to the battle ground the conflict was terminated and they were reluctantly forced to counter march. Little of consequence occurred on the twenty-first, and the next day saw the invaders planting batteries with which to reduce the city. At the same time rumors of peace were in the air.

These rumors were not without foundation, for the real purpose of the United States was to establish peace as soon as possible. President Polk had early expressed his desire to negotiate whenever the Mexicans would consent to do so.

Mexico, strengthened by the encouragement of many European newspapers and reports of a Whig revolution in Washington against the war, was not inclined to lend an ear to Polk's overtures of peace, especially so when our Government wished to dispense with any discussion of the causes of the war.

In an effort to bring about some agreement, James Buchanan, secretary of state, had Nicholas P. Trist, chief clerk of the State Department, sent to Mexico to enter into negotiations with the Mexican Government to effect a cessation of hostilities. Although Trist reached Vera Cruz on May 6, Santa Anna was not disposed to discuss peace until after the defeat of his soldiers at Churubusco on August 20. Then he sent a despatch to Buchanan (which was shown to Trist) proposing the negotiations which had been requested so many times by the American government. Later an offer of a truce was sent to Scott which he considered unsatisfactory, but he did offer a short armistice. This offer Santa Anna was only too eager to accept, and on the twenty-fourth the armistice was duly ratified.

Such, in brief outline, is the story of the events which brought a temporary halt to the conflict. For Geary's opinion of the armistice, and it seems fairly typical of most men in the army, let us turn again to the diary.

Aug. 29. I have been quite negligent of late about my notes, inasmuch as I have permitted 7 days to pass away without some remark.

The principal general topics which have transpired in the interim are the following. The framing of an Armistice between the Mexican Government under Santa Anna, and Mr. Triste [Trist] of the American Army—The leading feature of this Armistice, which prevents the entrance of our army into the city is peculiarly obnoxious to nearly every individual of the Army.—Three Commissioners have also met Mr. Triste to form a treaty of Peace, and up to this time are said to be progressing very well with their work—Plenty of money is obtained from the city on drafts etc to support our army and to pay off the soldiers.—So eager are the Mexicans to procure our drafts that they even allow a percentage for them.—The exact number of killed and wounded in the recent battles on the part of the Americans is 1233. (so says Gen Scott)

Our mode of living for some time has been of the poorest kind. George, our cook, has become mean, being anxious to go home. he does nothing aright, and deserves to be well flagelated. —Our fare for the last 3 weeks has almost exclusively consisted of hard bread & poor, tough beef, which being poorly cooked made me sick for several days. Nothing else could be procured, as all the Indians had vamosed the country during the fighting and nearly every thing the poor creatures owned was eaten or destroyed by the soldiery which preceded us. However, now with the aid of good police and plenty of money they have been induced to come from a distance with plenty of marketing, though it is yet at an awfully high price.—Gen Worth's Division is encamped at Tacabaya [Tacubaya] near the city. Twiggs' & Pillows Divisions between us and him.—And our Volunteer Division is still in San Augustine. This town is most beautifully irrigated both by nature and art with crystal streams flowing in every direction. The water is pure and cold, and the best I have tasted in Mexico.—The good water and the abundance of fruit in this place has added greatly to the health of our troops. San Augustine is a place of great resort in Summer. The citizens of Mexico make it a kind of gambling Depot, of which vice the whole Mexican nation is peculiarly fond.—Rains, heavy thunder storms and lightning are the order of the day every eving—The view from every quarter is hemmed in and terminated with hills and mountains. This place is about 10 miles from the city. (Sunday) I can scarcely realize it—I have not heard a sermon or a prayer since I left old Pennsylvania. God protect and shield me from such a dangerous and sinful situation, and may I be speedily restored to the land where peace reigns and gospel truths abound. I will however say "Welcome sweet day of rest. That saw the Lord arise." and that it is the sweetest of the seven. —May the many prayers which are offered up this day in my behalf and for my continued safety be heard at the throne of Grace and be availing as they have been throughout my life from my youth up.—I have always put my trust in God at all times and especially in the hour of danger. He has never deceived nor deserted me, nor will he if I continue to rely upon his Almighty Arms.

Sept. 1st. This morning is rosy, pleasant, clear and bright.—The sun pours forth his golden beams from the bright, lofty, and snowy peaks of the East, and speeds forth its roseate beams into the far famed Valley of Mexico. The birds carol forth sweet notes, making the groves vocal with their music.—The air is odoriferous from Orange Groves, flowers & roses.—Every thing taken together here would make this valley a perfect paradise, but the confounded bad government, the low order of the inhabitants, and their ignorance destroy every feeling for good or pleasure. On the 31st of August our Regt was mustered for payment by Lieut. Lovell.—Some difficulty is expected with the Mexicans as they talk publicly of breaking the Armistice.—We are therefore ordered to hold ourselves in readiness to march to the city at a moments notice.—We are always ready.—This day being Gen Quitman's birth day all the field officers of his Division were invited to drink wine with him at his quarters. We accordingly went and took a little of his good old sherry which want [*sic*] bad to take.[1] After an hour's pleasant conversation and toasts, the party separated well pleased with their host.—The market of the place is gradually improving —but every thing is exceedingly dear, chickens are sold for $62\frac{1}{2}$c & 75c each readily—nearly every[thing] else in proportion.—When the men want a luxury, they steal a chicken, rob a bee hive, kill a "gutter snipe" or take any thing that comes within arms length, but some of them have been caught at dirty tricks and will have to pay the penalty . . . We are all very patiently awaiting the decision of the Commissioners with regard to peace. We either want the sword or peace but not both, as we at this time expect.

Sept. 2nd. This morning I took a stroll about the town, and found a new variety of Chestnut about 4 times as large as the Pa chestnut but with the taste and flavor of the red oak acorn. We call them the horse chestnut. There is very little game here as far as I can discover, except ducks about the lakes, and a large grey hare similar in all respects to the Mountain hare of Pennsylvania. The rocks and stones are all of volcanic origin (scoria) and are as porous as honey combs.—They are however hard and answer a very good purpose for building.—The smaller spalls being used in the mortar seams of the *adobe* (or dryed brick)

[1] Many years later, as Governor of Pennsylvania, Geary's public receptions were noted for their lack of alcoholic refreshments. He was then a total abstainer.

houses, and walls around the gardens and also for capping the same.—The soil in many places is composed almost entirely of volcanic ashes.—Prospects of *Peace* brighten to-day. Santa Anna is determined to "sink or swim, survive or perish" with it, and his great influence may enable him to carry it through.—Upon our arrival here we found many of the citizens of Mexico, who had left the city and sought this place as a refuge. they soon afterward went to the city, and again returned, putting more confidence in their enemies than their friends. they believe themselves safer in our hands than in their own.

The rainy season is beginning to slack off and in about 4 weeks we expect to be clear of it.—Col Roberts is very sick with fever and spitting of blood. Robert McGinley is also sick of a fever in my quarters. I have attended on him for a number of days. he is some better. Many of the men in our Regiment have the dysentery and are beginning to die of it.—Corn soup & bread and beef are the standing diet of our Mess.—No variety.—I do not wonder that the children of Israel longed after the fleshpots of Egypt.

Sept 3. I am Officer of the Day—I make two tours, and visit all the pickets. The day is fine and clear. My friend R. M. McGinley is very low. he made sundry requests of me in case of his death which should he die and I live it will be my solemn duty to perform. Col Roberts is still unwell—he cannot sleep on account of smothering sensations. There is no news about the prospects of peace or war. Wrote to Edward. Opened my wife's letter and enclosed a red and a white rose.

Sept 4th & 5th. Fine and fair weather during the day, but rainy at night. Nothing of importance occurs. Col Roberts very sick. Since writing the above 3 of the soldiers of our Regt died.

Sept. 6. Probabilities are now rather in favor of the breaking of the Armistice on the part of the Mexicans. Our Division is ordered to be ready to move at a minutes warning, with 2 days provision.[1] We [are] expecting to-morrow morning to march to the City of Mexico. I am beginning to be pleased with San

[1] The peace negotiations conducted by four able Mexicans, appointees of Santa Anna, and Trist, who represented the United States, did not proceed satisfactorily. When Santa Anna became convinced that Trist intended to persist in his demand that Mexico accept the Rio Grande boundary, as well as give up New Mexico and upper California, he broke the armistice by strengthening the city's fortifications. On September 6 further parleying was abandoned. The war was to continue, and Scott knew that Mexico City would have to be captured.

Augustine, and if it was not for the excitement of seeing the big city I would be sorry to move our quarters. Marketing is very high—Chickens $1.00—Potatoes about the size of a nutmeg about 1¢ each. Butter $1.00 *per libra*—Manteca and media Peso per libra. All kinds of fruit are abundant and cheap—cheese 1½¢ per bite—Brandy $3.00 p.B Gin $3.00 per bottle. Ham 75¢ per libra. Lt Col Watson having declined, Gen Shields is appointed Governor of this place.

Sept 7th. Considerable excitement among the men of our Division to day on account of having been paid off—they received 6 months pay and a commutation for 2 mos clothing—generally amounting to near $50. per man. The Armistice is said to be broken, and we are now under orders to march for the city to-morrow at 7 oclock A.M. Col Roberts is still unwell, and the command of the 2nd Pennas will devolve on me. Nearly all the wounded were sent away to day.

Sept 8th. In accordance with orders we leave San Augustine, after a tedious delay in the morning on account of the trouble and difficulty of moving the sick and wounded. We get off about 9 oclock in the forenoon, carrying with us about 2000 Mexican prisoners. We passed through San Antonia where the Mexicans had at first made a decided stand, and where the gallant Thornton had been killed in reconoitering by a cannon ball.

We encamped in the eving in San Angel a village about 5 miles from San Augustine, and composed of the common adobe houses. This morning a severe action took place near the city—A foundry and a battery were taken from the enemy, together with a large amount of ammunition, provisions etc. Also six cannons newly cast.[1]

Our loss was 400 killed and wounded—Among the killed is Cols Graham & McIntosh & Lieut Rich Johnston. Col Roberts and McGinley are sent to the hospital near Tacabaya.

Sept. 9th. We lay all last night and this day expecting an order to march, but thus far have not received any such orders. I visited Col Roberts and found him poorly. Richard McMichael is appointed Lieut of Co "A" & Geo W Todd Sergeant Major of the Regt. Nothing of importance occurred.

---

[1] The engagement here referred to took place at El Molino del Rey (the King's Mill), which consisted of stone buildings lying about half a mile west of the fortified hill of Chapultepec. Unexpected difficulty was encountered in expelling the Mexicans from this position.

Sept 10th. This day I saw sights, not military parades, which usually take place at our loved homes, but a military execution of 16 prisoners. (deserters from our army and who joined the Mexicans and fought against us [at the battle of Churubusco] and killed many of our valuable officers) they were all hung upon the same gallows at the same time in a row—They all had white caps drawn over their faces and presented a singular appearance, such an one as perhaps may never be witnessed in my life time. The deserters were all Irishmen, and had deserted from Gen Taylors army. The circumstances of their high and vicious crimes being vividly before my imagination—their execution made no impression upon my mind whatever, not the least pity excited my breast. The principal hangman was a North of England man and he performed his duties with a peculiar relish and gusto.—Thirteen others were whipped with 50 stripes well laid on by a Mexican Muleteer—and branded on the right cheek with the letter "D" for deserter. they are to be chained and kept to the close of the war, carried to the U.S. and drummed through the different regts. The celebrated Maj. O Reilly was among these, he received an extra lash.—We were all day in expectation of marching orders but were again ordered to unload our waggons and remain over night in our present quarters. A guerrilla party has already taken possession of San Antonia. Santa Anna sent Gen Scott word to day to surrender his whole army into his (Santa Annas care) for safe keeping, as it would be impossible for him to restrain any longer the Army and the populace from cutting all our throats.

On September 11 Geary directed his men to fill their haversacks with provisions sufficient to last forty-eight hours. At five o'clock in the afternoon they started for Tacubaya and arrived there just before dawn. The great towers and porcelain domes of the Capital now met their eyes.

To take Mexico City Scott knew that his plan of attack must of necessity be tempered with caution, for the losses sustained by his army in the previous battles around the city had made serious inroads on its strength. After the territory had been thoroughly investigated he called a meeting of his generals and engineers on the morning of September 11 to decide on the point of attack. When he had heard the various opinions of his officers, Scott declared himself to be in favor of striking at the western side of the city.

As the formidable hill of Chapultepec lay on this side, capped by strongly fortified buildings, its elimination would be necessary before the city itself could be reached. To accomplish this Scott began placing his artillery in the most effective positions.

On the twelfth all batteries were soon in order and a heavy fire was directed at the Castle of Chapultepec. This fortress, situated at the top of a precipitous hill 150 feet high and protected at the bottom by the cream of the Mexican artillery, was probably the greatest obstruction encountered by the army. Here the Second Pennsylvania was to see its bitterest fighting.

On the morning of the thirteenth Scott, realizing that a direct assault would be necessary, gave the command to advance on the frowning stronghold. Quitman's command attacked from the southeast, over the Tacubaya causeway in the face of a terrific fire from the outworks at the base of the hill. Encountering a veritable hail of lead, his troops advanced over the rough swampy land to within two hundred yards of the annihilating batteries. Those who had been assigned as stormers were making but little progress, when Quitman sent General Shields with the New York and South Carolina regiments and the Second Pennsylvania under Geary to advance obliquely on the left and breach the wall at the foot of the hill, and thus aid the assault of the stormers on that flank. The volunteers plunged through the morass to aid the stormers who were waiting under the ruins. The deluge of lead could not halt these cheering men. Five balls pierced Geary's uniform, and finally he was struck in the groin by a spent canister ball. Of this wound one of his men, William J. Ivory, wrote: "I saw him at the time and thought he was gone, but the wound turned out to be trifling, as he was with us when we got into the Castle."

After the fortress had fallen, Quitman, using the discretionary powers given him by Scott before the battle began, ordered his men on to the city. Here the Second Pennsylvania did heroic work at the Garita de Belen, a gate on the southwest. The men were caught in a destructive enfilading fire, but nothing daunted, pressed forward. At 1:20 o'clock in the afternoon Quitman's impetuous charge carried him to the batteries at the gate. The troops then rushed past the gate but were recalled until batteries could be constructed to back the proposed attack upon the citadel, an extensive, well-protected structure, from which the guns were still blazing away.

A renewal of the attack was not necessary, however, for on the next morning a white flag announced the citadel's surrender. This was tantamount to a surrender of the whole city. The boys from Pennsylvania now trod the proud and ancient halls of the Montezumas.

Later, upon looking back at that bloody day which brought Mexico City to its knees, Geary could be justifiably proud of the gallant conduct of the troops under his command. The Second Pennsylvania was first within the walls of Mexico City, and Lebbeus Allshouse, of Westmoreland County, a member of the regiment, was the first man to scale the ramparts at Chapultepec.

For the Lieutenant Colonel's impression of the fight, let us take a leaf from his diary:

Sept. 13th. During the night [of the 12th] a large portion of the troops were employed in constructing a new breastworks. Early in the morning orders were given to prepare to storm the fortress, and about 7 oclock all were ready and the storm began. I need not here pretend to give a description of the battle, for I would be totally inadequate to the task. Suffice it to say I was wounded about the middle of the action, but had an opportunity of witnessing the whole of the action. The fight was the most brilliant of the war, and the 2nd Pennsylvania Reg't came out "A no. 1." In a few minutes of the taking of the fortress, we were again ordered forward in pursuit of the enemy, which I was able to lead, having nearly recovered from my contusion. The fire of the enemy was dreadful while we took the gates of San Cosme and Tacubaya, into the City of Mexico. After fighting all day and working nearly all night, we lay down for an hour or two, expecting to renew the conflict—more hotly than ever in the morning.

Sept 14. We were aroused early this morning and put in battle array expecting every moment to receive an iron hail storm from the enemy—but after waiting half an hour, judge our surprise to see a white flag approaching announcing the surrender of the citadel, the strongest military work in the city. This was of course equivalent to surrendering the city. So it proved. I was placed in command of the citadel with my regiment as a mark of dignity for good behavior the day previous.

Thus in these few words Geary modestly describes his part in one of the greatest feats of soldiering ever performed by an army anywhere. No boasting or self-commendation, just a simple account of the facts. A real soldier, but without the usual soldier's flair for braggadocio.

After a few days the new commander of the citadel recovered from his painful wound and marched his men into the Capital. The soldiers were stationed in the University, while he found quarters in the Palace.

On October 2 the city was jarred by a terrific earthquake, the worst since 1844, lasting two minutes and four seconds. "The waving of the ground," wrote Geary, "the shaking of the trees to and fro and the agitation of the water were sights to me of rare curiosity, and must say of pleasure. [Apparently Geary was not well pleased with Mexico City.] The Castle was rent from the top to the bottom and across the roof." He describes the water as running "in the gutters, first up then downhill. . . . The house I occupied during the shock rocked like a cradle." It must have been quite an experience for a man coming from a land where the hills had stood in unshakable serenity for countless ages.

On the next day Geary sadly recounts the death of Colonel Roberts. The former had been performing the duties of a colonel for several weeks prior to Roberts' death. On November 3 his untiring vigilance and efficiency throughout the entire campaign were rewarded by his own men when they elected him colonel with a vote of 256 to his nearest competitor's 152. Major Brindle was elected lieutenant colonel.

Time goes by rapidly for the new Colonel, and little of consequence occurs that seems worthy to record. On February 6 he says: "Rumors of peace are still rife." And on February 10 he makes the last entry in his diary. With exception of one last page the little green book was full. How we regret this, for his detailed information, musings, and observations are enjoyable as well as invaluable to the student of the history of this period.

Up to the date of his last entry Geary had apparently known nothing about the treaty of peace which was signed at Guadalupe Hidalgo between the United States and Mexico on February 2, 1848. Although Trist's authority had been removed by Polk he nevertheless took part in the negotiations.

After peace was definitely established the soldiers in Mexico received orders to depart for the United States. This was gladly complied with, for the American troops were ready and eager to go back home.

The return trip was a long one, but when the travel-stained and weary Second Pennsylvania Regiment arrived at Pittsburgh on the steamer *Taglioni*, a tremendous ovation awaited it. They were the first men to arrive from the field of war, and the populace did them full justice. The streets were lined with rejoicing people; bells were rung, guns were fired, and the usual long adjectival speeches were made.

Geary's record in the Mexican War was one of which any man might be proud. He had served efficiently and bravely, earning the hearty commendation of his superior officers and the respect of his men. But usually, when a man has earned an enviable reputation in the advancement of a cause, there are always those of a jealous nature who attempt to undermine his good standing in the eyes of his fellow men. Geary was no exception. Without the slightest chance to defend himself, he became the target of a malicious and unjustified attack which caused him considerable worry and embarrassment. Samuel H. Montgomery, a quartermaster from Westmoreland County, in a letter to a Greensburg paper, caused all the trouble. He alleged that the Second Pennsylvania was poorly officered, that it did not fight in the battles of Contreras and Churubusco because its officers could not be found when wanted. He further hinted that Geary and Roberts tried to avoid battles because of fear. This was a rascally attack and entirely unfounded, having no factual basis whatever, as will be immediately shown.

Senator Simon Cameron and Representative James Thompson, both of Pennsylvania, heard the spiteful rumor being circulated, and in an attempt to discover its truth or falsity, asked General Quitman for the facts. Quitman replied by letter as follows:

I have not seen the publications in relation to the officers of the Second Pennsylvania Regiment, to which you alluded in our conversation of yesterday; I am, however, informed that these publications charge the field officers of that gallant regiment with backwardness, or a reluctance to participate in the battle of Contreras.

Justice to the late lamented Colonel Roberts, and to Lieutenant-Colonel Geary and Major Brindle, both of whom acted with distinguished credit in the subsequent severe and bloody contests at Chapultepec and at the gates of the City of Mexico, requires me, as their immediate commander to state that there is not the least foundation for such an imputation.

He then declares that Geary "solicited that his regiment might be designated for the movement in advance."

Quartermaster Montgomery's mendacious imputations become absurdly ridiculous when we learn directly from Quitman in the above statement that Geary *requested* the advance position in the fighting around Mexico City. This hardly sounds like the request of a man who was reluctant to fight.

Furthermore, General Scott in his official report says that the Second Pennsylvania was detailed to guard the siege, supply, and baggage trains. "If these," he declares, "had been lost, the army would have been driven almost to despair; and considering the enemy's very great excess of numbers and the many approaches to the depot, it might well have become, emphatically, the *post of honor*."

Thus we see that the Second Pennsylvania was kept out of the preliminary battles at Mexico City for an excellent reason; and it is inconceivable that a commanding general of Scott's sagacity would delegate a poorly officered regiment to a position that might have become "the post of honor."

When news of the slander reached the regiment itself, twenty-eight captains and lieutenants immediately prepared a denial of the charge, which appeared in the Bedford *Gazette*. In referring to Montgomery's accusation they said: "The deed could only have been prompted by imbecility, and sentiments infinitely removed from those of a noble nature."

They continue: "It affords us pleasure to add that the Second Pennsylvania Regiment is commanded by officers of ability, bravery, and intelligence, and that we are not guilty of promoting men who were ever known to deviate from the paths of rectitude and honor."

It is to be perceived from the above refutations that Montgomery's accusation was utterly false. Yet its insinuations pursued Geary for a long time.

III

POSTMASTER OF SAN FRANCISCO

COLONEL GEARY had been back in Pennsylvania only a short time when Polk, on January 22, 1849, appointed him postmaster of San Francisco. He was furnished with powers to appoint postmasters, create post-offices, make contracts for carrying the mails throughout California, and establish mail routes, as many and in such places as he deemed advisable.

How the Colonel obtained this appointment is a matter of conjecture. Since there is no evidence of the intercession of friends on his behalf, it seems quite clear that he obtained the appointment chiefly on his own initiative, strengthened considerably by the President's grateful recognition of his faithful service in Mexico. Regardless of all this, the fact remains that he had gone to Washington, and on his return brought the appointment with him.

With characteristic energy and zeal he prepared for the long and arduous trip to California. This land of El Dorado could be reached in a variety of ways, but the three most popular were "around the Horn," "by way of the Isthmus," or across the plains. The first route was usually preferred by the seafaring New Englanders, and required from six to nine months. The path over the plains was difficult, and was usually selected by families of hardy pioneers who set out in long winding strings of covered wagons, or "prairie schooners." The route across the Isthmus was the shortest and quickest of the three, under favorable circumstances. The distance from New York to Chagres was 2,500 miles; from Chagres to Panama, sixty miles; from Panama to San Francisco, 3,500 miles. No matter which route the traveler selected, it was bound to be fraught with peril, discomfort, and hardship: heat and Indians on the plains; nautical perils at Cape Horn; fever and aimless natives on the Isthmus.

Geary selected the Isthmus route as the best and quickest. On

February 1, 1849, he sailed with his wife and son, Edward, from New York on board the *Falcon*, bound for Chagres.

Sea passage to California in those days was decidedly adventurous, and proportionately uncomfortable. Navigation clerks promised everything and guaranteed nothing. As the demand for transportation increased, every boat that could cut a wave was put into service. Old leaky tubs, built for anything but the passenger's comfort and convenience, plied back and forth on indeterminate runs from the Atlantic ports to California.

The *Falcon*, overloaded with 317 passengers and badly equipped, was typical of the lot. The greatest diversity of individuals imaginable crowded the deck and jammed pell-mell into the dining room. Laborers, politicians, clerks, ministers, and gamblers mingled indiscriminately and loudly talked of the good fortune that most certainly awaited them, one and all, when their golden destination was reached. Most of them assumed the picturesque garb of the prospector: soft, flapping broad-brimmed hats, heavy boots, bowie knives, brass-studded boots, and vivid red shirts. Most were happy and good natured, all were hopeful, as they talked of the waiting riches and of the impracticable mining machines which littered the deck.

At last the steamer's destination was reached. For those who had never seen a tropical port the little village of Chagres presented a bizarre and unusual appearance. Nude, dark-skinned children romped about through acres of mud, filth, and refuse. Everywhere piles of rubbish decomposed uninterruptedly, lending a poignant stench to the heavy air. Men and women in varying stages of undress lolled under the trees or huts, gazing somnolently at these hurrying Northerners who demanded everything with such meaningless haste. The one hotel, the Crescent City, possessed mud floors and no food, but was abundantly supplied with fleas and cockroaches.

As the passengers descended en masse upon the little malodorous town of cane huts to secure transportation up the river, competition waxed keen and bitter. Good fellowship was forgotten. "Every man for himself and the devil take the hindmost" became the slogan. Lethargic and indifferent, the natives refused to be hurried. What was the use? Passengers abounded, boats were few, and almost any price asked was granted.

Once disembarked, Geary and some fellow passengers formed a committee to devise a means of crossing the Isthmus. After considerable haggling the steamer *Orus* was secured to take them to Gorgona at eleven dollars per person. By land the distance from Chagres to Gorgona was twenty-four miles, but by the river, which meandered in every direction, the miles increased to fifty. With one-half of the *Falcon's* passengers aboard, the *Orus* started on her way; but when only nineteen miles had been covered, their captain informed them that further passage up the river was impossible for a boat as large as the *Orus*. They then resorted to canoes, about one of which Geary writes to General G. W. Bowman: "A large half covered 'dug-out,' about 30 feet long and 3 feet wide, with a crew of 5 negroes was allotted to Captain Simons, myself, and our two ladies."

At that time no accommodations were provided along the route, and travelers had to fare as best they could. On the third day out the little party's supply of food was exhausted, and the hostile inhabitants living along the river refused to sell them any. Geary, resolved to obtain food by some means, went ashore and shot two chickens, throwing the owner a dollar in payment. The money amply covered the value of the birds, but the angry owner and two of his friends rushed toward the Colonel, brandishing huge clubs. They were almost upon him when he aimed his pistol, and told them he had four shots left. Another step would most certainly bring their death. Awed by their opponent's size and evident determination, they halted to allow Geary to walk slowly away, still carrying his chickens. This encounter had happened on a little peninsula which jutted out into the river. Now he went to the other side of this stretch of land, still keeping his assailants at bay. Finally they decided to leave, no doubt believing that it would be much safer to accept the dollar and let the matter drop. The victor now cooked his quarry with the aid of some utensils he was lucky enough to find there, and when his party arrived in the boat they all had a hearty and much-needed meal.

That third night was one of intense physical discomfort. Their unreliable boatmen had deserted, leaving the party on the banks of the Chagres River, surrounded by jungle beasts and deluged by a sweeping tropical rain. The two men alternated at keeping watch on the shore, listening to night prowlers thrashing about in the water and the bushes, while the rest of the group found partial shelter in the canoe.

On the evening of the next day, February 17, they arrived, tired and weary, at Gorgona.

To quote again from Geary's letter to General Bowman, he advises travelers "to bring with them Mexican dollars and five franc pieces in any quantity; they pass here for $1.25 each. Bring also as many ten cent pieces as may be convenient, eight of them pass for a dollar."

They left Gorgona the next day, via mules, and set out along the trail for Panama, twenty-two miles away. To Geary the trail was not so bad as many writers had pictured it. True, innumerable dead mules attracted the usual flocks of vultures, and muddy water squirted from under the mules' hoofs in a spray; but all in all the road was rather pleasant.

Mrs. Geary, who in her husband's opinion was "probably the first lady who has crossed the Isthmus without riding Spanish fashion," experienced little discomfort during the seven and one-half hours' journey. The party reached its destination in the evening. Now it was necessary to wait for the steamer *Oregon*, which was coming around the Horn on its way to San Francisco.

This wait at Panama was one of the great disadvantages of the Isthmus route. As there were more ships on the Atlantic than on the Pacific coast, travelers were forced to stay at Panama City over long periods until a boat to the north would arrive. Although a prompt through passage was promised by the shipping officials, that promise was rarely if ever realized.

The stay at Panama was not a pleasant one; sickness and privation were common among the many people who had gathered there after traversing the Isthmus. Geary, never content with idleness, was moved by a kindly nature to do something which would alleviate the sufferings of his fellow wayfarers. Accordingly he created a Masonic society and an Odd Fellows organization. These societies proved to be a great help to future travelers. He also, in conjunction with several other men, assisted in the publication of the first American newspaper ever to be printed in English in that locality.

While in Panama the Colonel had a little adventure which bears repeating, because it so admirably illustrates his character. One morning he awoke to discover that he had been robbed of several articles during the night. He immediately went to the guardhouse, where he asked the sergeant and the twelve men under him for information concerning the possible perpetrators of the theft. From the moment he entered their presence they acted in a peculiar and suspicious manner. Although understanding his Spanish well enough, they denied their ability to do so. They asked him insulting questions, and made threatening demonstrations with their side arms. Finally one of the soldiers struck him a painful blow on the ear. In spite of being outnumbered thirteen to one, Geary was in no mood to take this last indignity. Striking out with the full force of his weight he caught the offender neatly on the jaw. The man did not remain in a conscious state long enough to regret his hastiness, for at the impact of the blow he sank limply to the floor and passed temporarily from the scene of combat. Twelve vicious characters still remained, however, making the situation extremely desperate. Blows rained on him, but he charged through the remaining guardsmen with all the speed of an infuriated bull. It is little wonder that his assailants recoiled from those huge flailing arms, for their owner weighed approximately two hundred and sixty pounds and stood six feet five inches high in his bare feet. Through an open door he saw a row of muskets standing in the guardroom. Realizing the urgent necessity of getting a weapon in his hands he raced to the muskets, secured one, and roared that he would shoot the first man to touch him. His adversaries now stood hesitantly about, not relishing the idea of an open attack on this iron-jawed giant who had proved so formidable. One man now attempted a ruse. He came close, threw himself on a pile of blankets and attempted to trip the Colonel. Geary sidestepped, grabbed his tormentor's bayonet from its scabbard and placed it on his musket. On the fellow's second attempt to dislodge him from his position in front of the guns, Geary stabbed him in the leg, and picking him up, blanket and all, threw him out of the door. There on the floor lay the stolen equipment. This sudden revelation of their guilt cowed the men. They immediately became subservient to their intended victim's wishes, and carried the stolen property to its rightful place.

Back in his own quarters Geary checked his property. Satisfied that it had all been restored, he gave the gun which he had brought along from the guardroom to the last soldier, and then kicked him down the stairs.

Later in the day Geary got in touch with the American consul and the military commandant. A trial was immediately ordered by the latter, and the culprits found guilty. On the following day they received fifty lashes on their bare backs in the public square.

The little party had been in Panama, along with more than a thousand other travelers, thirty-four days when the *Oregon* finally arrived. It took the marooned wayfarers on board on April 13, and proceeded uneventfully up the coast to discharge its 350 passengers at their final destination.

At last they were in San Francisco, that amazing and riotous city where fabulous sums were being made and lost every day. It was San Francisco of the gold-rush days, the stirring times of '49, when the wheel of fortune whirled crazily, but constantly.

From a drowsy little town of two hundred souls in 1846, San Francisco had, in three surprising years, grown into a densely populated city of feverish activity. Like Rip Van Winkle, the little hamlet had awakened over night to enter a strange world. With the magic cry of GOLD! GOLD! the village was almost drained of its citizens; but their place was taken by multitudes. During the first six months of 1849 over ten thousand people came into town. Other thousands followed. Its fame spread to all parts of the world, carried by the excited press of near and distant cities, by the tongues of wildly gesticulating men. From all climes and all walks of life they came, the greed of gold ever in their eyes.

> Englishmen and French,
> German, Dutch and Danish,
> Chattering Chinese,
> Portuguese and Spanish;
> Men of every nation,
> Birds of every feather,
> Honest men and rogues
> Hustled up together.[1]

The town was young, the visitors were young; and typical of youthful enthusiasm, they grew lustily together. With unprecedented speed the few houses multiplied and spread haphazardly over the sands; a forest of masts, as if summoned by Aladdin's wonderful lamp, appeared in the harbor. Building supplies sold at unbelievable figures, and rents were tremendous. Forty thousand dollars a year for the meanest of shelters was common.

As was to be expected, law and order were strangers. Every man was a law unto himself. Hold-ups and petty thievery were common; dueling was the order of the day, for one's "honor" was a very touchy thing indeed. Many a peaceful game of poker ended with the explosion of guns and flashing of knives. Gambling halls and saloons grew thick as flies on the city's most prominent spots. Gambling, far from being the furtive thing it is today, flourished unhindered. It was a big business in the full

[1] Rockwell D. Hunt and Nellie Van de Grift Sanchez, *A Short History of California*, Thomas Y. Crowell Co. (New York, 1929), p. 431.

sense of the word, for almost everyone gambled. The doors of the El Dorado, one of the coast's most famous halls of chance, never stopped swinging, day or night.

The streets, in spite of their being either suffocatingly thick with dust, or at other times "hands over head" deep in mud, were always covered with hurrying throngs. Everybody was busy, everybody was doing something, nefarious or otherwise.

The new Postmaster stepped off the gangplank on that warm spring day for his first close look at this chaotic city of shacks and gold. The shortage of labor was immediately made evident when he inquired for somebody to carry his trunks. Upon being informed that his luggage could be conveyed for not less than five dollars a piece, Geary exclaimed at the exorbitant price and carried the baggage himself.

The new post-office, which housed the first regular mail from the Atlantic states to be opened in San Francisco, was located on the corner of Montgomery and Washington streets in a small room, woefully lacking in all the appointments required for such an undertaking. With energetic zeal Uncle Sam's new appointee busily set to work in an effort to distribute the five thousand letters entrusted to his care. Assistants were employed for sixteen dollars a day, alphabetized squares were drawn on the floor to serve as boxes, and the room's one window acted as a delivery vent when one of its panes was removed. The office was soon declared officially open for business, and the populace swarmed down to receive its long-anticipated mail. This was an important and gala occasion, for some of the residents had not received Eastern mail for months. Men stood in line for hours, and the highly prized positions near the head of the line sold for as much as sixteen dollars.

The Postmaster's tireless efforts soon brought order out of chaos, and the little office began to function smoothly. The need for larger quarters caused Geary to change its location to the intersection of Washington and Stockton streets, and then to the corner of Clay and Pike streets, where it stayed for some time.

But just when his well-laid plans were bearing fruit, he was removed from office in favor of Jacob Moore by General Taylor, who had just become President of the United States. Resolved not to hold his job a day longer than necessary, he asked Colonel Allen, mail agent for California, to release him from his duties. The request being granted, Colonel Bryan was appointed to take over the postmastership until the arrival of Moore.

Geary was now undecided as to his future course. He saw the possibilities of San Francisco, but he was also fully cognizant of the fact that the city, terrorized by the "Hounds" (a band of cut-throats, calling themselves the "Regulators"), was no place for his wife, who was unfortunately in delicate health. In April she had given birth to a second son, William L. Geary, who was the first male child born in San Francisco after the cession of California to the United States. Believing it best for their health and safety, he sent the members of his family back to Pennsylvania. Realizing the golden business opportunities in San Francisco, he formed a partnership with William Van Voorhees and O. P. Sutton to enter into a general auction and commission business under the name of Geary, Van Voorhees and Sutton.

About this time the Governor of California, General Riley, felt the need of a man to fill the office of alcalde (similar to our mayor) which had recently become vacant. The alcalde's duties required him to settle matters of a public and private nature, and also to keep a watchful eye on the morals of the town, not an inconsiderable task in the ebullient San Francisco of those days. Consequently Riley ordered an election to take place on August 1. Although Geary had consistently refused to run for office, he discovered to his amazement that his name had been placed on all the ten different tickets for first alcalde, and that he had won the office by a unanimous total vote of 1,516. In attestation of this, Frederick Billings, chairman of the Board of Inspectors and Judges, sent the following notice to the new Alcalde:

To Hon. JOHN W. GEARY:—

At a special election held in San Francisco, August 1st, 1849, to fill the vacancy existing in the office of First Alcalde of said town and district, you were elected by fifteen hundred and sixteen votes, being the whole number cast.

FREDERICK BILLINGS
Chairman Bd. Inspectors and Judges
San Francisco, August 2nd, 1849.

In an address made to the Ayuntamiento [1] following the election, First Alcalde Geary painted a clear and realistic picture of the situation then existing in the city. He stressed the heavy obligation which rested on their shoulders, asked their full co-operation, and promised that in return for the overwhelming vote of confidence it had been his honor to receive, he would "cause the observance of every law and ordinance made for the good of the city."

Undoubtedly the new but violently robust town was suffering from severe growing pains. The Alcalde was well aware of this, and if he stressed the bad conditions at considerable length, he was nevertheless facing the true facts as they existed.

At this time [he said] we are without a dollar in the public treasury, and it is to be feared the city is greatly in debt. You have neither an office for your magistrate, nor any other public edifice. You are without a single police officer or watchman, and have not the means of confining a prisoner for an hour. . . . Public improvements are unknown in San Francisco. In short you are without a single requisite for the promotion of prosperity, for the protection of property, or for the maintenance of order.

The situation was indeed gloomy. To remedy it required money. The new Alcalde now demanded that a tax be levied not only on property, but on auction sales as well. Merchants, traders, and boat owners were required to take out a license.

[1] The Ayuntamiento, or town council, had numerous and important duties to perform. Under Spanish rule it had authority over all public business in the town, and this authority was often extended over the district in which the town was located.

Gaming and billiard tables were also to be licensed until state
legislation on the subject could be enacted.

The speaker concluded by strongly recommending the cause
of education:

The laws under which we act oblige each officer, without
regard to his station, to advance, with his utmost zeal, the cause
of education. I, therefore, strongly urge upon you the propriety of adopting measures by which the children of the high,
the low, the rich and poor of this district, can have equal ad-
vantages of drinking freely at the fountain of primary knowledge; and it is to be hoped that our territory which is ere long
to be erected into a State, and placed by the side of her elder
sisters of the Union, will show to them that she fully appreciates
education as the only safeguard of our republican Institutions. . . .

Thus, only a few days after resigning his postmastership—
eight, to be exact—the Colonel found himself in a highly responsible position. His duties were many and onerous: he was sheriff,
probate judge, recorder, notary public, and coroner, as well as
judge of first instance. He had been appointed to this last position, shortly after the election, by Governor Riley. In addition
to all this, he was elected president of the Democratic party's
association in San Francisco. The latter honor was conferred
upon him on October 21.

Geary's overwhelming success in the election, and his subsequent important appointments were considered by many to
be a direct blow at the judgment of the national administration
which had removed him. Sample Flinn, in a letter to his brother,
declares that Geary "is one of the most popular men in this
country. . . . His triumphant and popular election is a severe
and just rebuke to the reckless administration at Washington."
He makes a significant remark on the condition of politics in
California when he says: "More than half the population here
are Democrats, although party lines are not yet fairly drawn."

It was in the month of September that the Constitutional
Convention at Monterey signed the finished document. Al-

though Geary's duties prevented him from being a delegate at this convention, he was highly influential in inserting the free-state clause into California's state constitution. This pretty well indicates his views on slavery.

Alcalde Geary soon realized the demands made in his inaugural speech. On August 27, the Ayuntamiento placed a percentage duty on sales of real estate and merchandise. Later, license duties were placed on those engaged in various businesses. Particularly lucrative were the duties collected from gambling, an activity that continued to thrive mightily and unrestrained. To provide a place of confinement for criminals, the Council purchased the brig *Euphemia*, which served admirably.

San Francisco was about as lawless as was possible for a place to be and still maintain a semblance of organized government. Drunkenness, rioting, murder, and theft were the order of the day. Toward the end of 1849, from twenty to twenty-five thousand people lived in the city without a single peace officer to control them.

The Judge of First Instance had an enormous task on his hands. According to the *Annals of San Francisco*,

> He daily held an ordinary police or mayor's court, an alcalde's court for the minor cases and general executive matters of the city; a court of first instance with universal civil jurisdiction; a court of first instance with like criminal extent; and a court of admiralty for maritime cases. In fine, he was the Curator of the Public, doing everything that was to be done, even to the holding of inquests and taking acknowledgment of deeds.

Although the Alcalde's duties were burdensome and many, the compensation for his services was not inconsiderable. The *Alta California* for January 4, 1850, states that his salary was "higher than that received by the President of the United States."

Work piled up with such rapidity that Geary was forced to ask for another magistrate to relieve him of some of his duties. As a result, William B. Almond was made judge of first instance, with civil jurisdiction only. Almond was quite a singular character. In the course of a hearing he would often sit behind the bench, occupied in trimming his fingernails or paring a troublesome corn. To hear both sides of certain cases was a flagrant waste of time. He formed an opinion, regardless of the number of witnesses heard, and issued a verdict, then and there. This was hardly in accordance with regular court procedure, but it was fast. That, to Almond, was the end in view—arbitrary but effective.

On January 8 another election was held. This time it was for the purpose of electing an alcalde and members of the Legislature and ayuntamiento. The highest vote cast was for Geary, who was again running for alcalde: 3,425 votes in his favor with only twelve for other candidates. Such an overwhelming popular endorsement spoke well for his previous term of office.

Geary was equally popular as judge of first instance. While in office he heard 2,500 cases. Of this number only twelve were appealed, and none of these were ever reversed. Simple confinement was thought too easy for many criminals, so to discourage future crime, and to materially aid the city as well, Geary organized the vicious characters into a chain gang to repair the streets.

Always interested in education, the Alcalde established the city's first public school, to educate and deter youth from crime. He also served as President of the State and City Boards of Health in an effort to stamp out cholera.

IV

MAYOR OF SAN FRANCISCO

In 1850 San Francisco departed from the Mexican system of government to adopt the American municipal system. Dissatisfaction with the old form was general and oft expressed. In the tri-weekly *Alta California* of January 11, 1850, is a typical statement of the deprecation in which it was held by the citizens:

Ever since their election, the Prefect and Alcalde and Ayuntamiento have been constantly at loggerheads, and disagreeing upon most important subjects. We hope that we shall soon be rid of everything that smacks of Mexican law, and that the Ayuntamiento, Alcaldes, Prefects and high constables will all be done away with.

The above-mentioned conflict between the Prefect, Ayuntamiento, and Alcalde grew bitter as well as amusing. The Prefect, Horace Hawkes, accused the Ayuntamiento and Geary, alcalde at the time, of assuming illegal and arbitrary powers, while the accused parties retaliated in like manner. The nature of the quarrel is well illustrated in two letters which passed between Geary and Hawkes, extracts of which are quoted. Hawkes accuses Geary of "taking cognizance of civil causes where the amount exceeds 100 dollars and even of arresting and imprisoning parties in civil cases. This you have no right to do," Horace declares, "and if you attempt to do it, your orders and processes are *absolutely null and void*, and no man is bound to obey you." He concludes his communication by demanding a reply. Heretofore Geary had failed to answer the Prefect's irate and indignant letters.

Geary replies, succinctly and to the point:

"You complain that I have been in the habit of treating your communications with contempt. I have the honor to inform you that 'your' communication of to-day is before me, it will soon be behind me." Just that and nothing more.

These letters clearly illustrate the friendliness, or lack of it, that existed in the municipal government of San Francisco just before the Mexican system expired.

With the demise of the old system, the first city charter was adopted; and in the elections that followed on April 30, Geary was elected mayor, defeating the Whig candidate, Charles J. Brenham, by a substantial majority.

In commenting on the event, the *Daily Pacific News*, of May 1, 1850, said:

Col. John W. Geary is the first mayor of the commercial metropolis of the Pacific, in spite of the lamentations here or elsewhere. This is an honor of which any man might be proud, and we congratulate our Democratic friends upon the result of their day's work. . . . The steamer to-day will take to the Atlantic the gratifying intelligence that California is a Democratic State.

In his first speech before the Council the new Mayor throws light upon the repeated devastation wrought by fires in San Francisco.

There is not a single well or pump upon any public street or square. . . . The circumstances attending the calamitous fires of the 4th instant and the 24th of December last, clearly prove that could a reasonable supply of water have been obtained, when the fires were first discovered, they would have been extinguished, even without the use of engines, before any material damage had occurred.

For improving and beautifying the city he suggests that Portsmouth Square be turned into a recreational center and the streets graded. As alcalde, Geary had shown a real interest in public improvements by paying from his own resources $3,200 to satisfy the laborers' demands for wages. For supplying water, grading the streets, and erecting public buildings, he suggested that the lowest-bidding contractors should be hired.

He also advised the Council to appoint a committee to decide on a course relative to the care of the sick and indigent. This was an important item, because during the last nine months the city had spent $80,000 in such work. He concluded his remarks by requesting that police and night watchmen be hired and the streets lighted with lamps.

Although San Francisco had experienced two bad fires before Geary took office, it was during his term that the greatest ones occurred. The citizens were too busy making money to comply immediately with his requests for fire-fighting equipment and adequate public sources of water supply. Time and again the business section was almost totally destroyed by these terrible conflagrations. The Mayor did everything in his power to prevent their occurrence, but the nature of the city's buildings was such that if one burst into flames, those adjacent did also. All being of cheap and flimsy construction, the fire, once started properly, soon became practically uncontrollable. The chief means of preventing a fire's spread lay in tearing down buildings so that the blaze might be allowed to burn itself out. While superintending the demolition of a building during one of the major fires, Geary was fired upon by its owner. Not hesitating a moment, he knocked the man down and proceeded with his work. Although threatened with death several times, he knew he was doing the sensible thing, and nothing could deter him. Later on the city was sued by property owners who had their buildings destroyed by gunpowder, but the courts ruled against the plaintiffs, stating that the demolition of structures was the only possible way of stopping the progress of fires.

The Mayor was also considerably annoyed by members of the Board of Aldermen. Against a solid wall of public disapproval they insisted that each of their members should receive a reimbursement of four thousand dollars a year. The Mayor supported the citizens, but against his wishes the aldermen promptly passed an ordinance to collect their salaries. The Mayor just as promptly vetoed the measure on the grounds that all available money would be required to meet the interest on a loan then being negotiated. Furthermore, he believed that the aldermen received sufficient recompense in the honor bestowed upon them by the electorate. Finally, the city was almost penniless. In view of these circumstances he felt that "retrenchment should be the order of the day, rather than the opening up of new modes of making enormous and heretofore unknown expenditures."

The veto was loudly applauded by the citizens, but the aldermen obstinately passed their ordinance over the executive's head. The matter remained in this position until the next year, when the State Legislature, in a new charter to the city, declared that in the future, members of the Common Council should receive no compensation for their services.

In November the Mayor again came into conflict with the aldermen; this time over the construction of a road under private enterprise from Kearney Street to the Mission Dolores. The aldermen approved of the proposed road, and passed an ordinance to that effect, but Geary vetoed it, believing that the road should be constructed by the city itself, since the road was to be sustained by toll collection. Colonel Wilson, the man who was sponsoring the project, appealed to the State Legislature. This body confirmed the ordinance of the City Council, and construction was immediately begun.

When election day again rolled around, Geary was presented with a communication signed by a large number of respectable citizens, requesting that he be a candidate for a second term as mayor. The request was refused, but shortly afterward he was named as a member of the Board of Commissioners of the Funded Debt, and when that body met he was elected its president.

The problem confronting the commissioners was a difficult one. The city was in debt to the sum of $1,500,000 at three per cent interest per month, aggregating $540,000 a year interest charges. The Board attempted to fund the debt by selling bonds which bore ten per cent per annum, payable in city scrip.

An act of the Legislature gave all the city lands to the Board in trust for the benefit of its creditors. Many of them now bought the bonds, but others insisted on a sheriff's sale of city property, in spite of the previous conveyance of city lands to the commissioners. Later the Supreme Court legalized the sheriff's sales, but the funding plan was nevertheless successful. The bonds rose from twenty-five per cent to their face value, including interest.

Having helped to bring the city's debt problem to a successful conclusion, Geary took a six months' leave of absence and returned to Pennsylvania. Here his wife's illness, from which she never recovered, held him in the East long past the intended six months. Later, because of further deaths of near relatives, and business activities, he decided to remain permanently in Pennsylvania and tend his farm. He never returned to California.

Geary's sojourn in San Francisco had been remarkably successful. As first United States postmaster, as alcalde, as judge of first instance, as mayor, and as chairman of the Board of Commissioners of the Funded Debt, he helped to shape the course not only of the famous city of San Francisco, but of California as well. Succeeding in governmental affairs, he was also fortunate in personal financial matters. His affiliation with Van Voorhees and Sutton was lucrative, but more so was his interest in real estate. On one day's sale of lots he realized $125,-000, and he was commonly reputed to have been worth half a million dollars, just before he left San Francisco. This was wealth, even in the land of El Dorado.

Now at the early age of thirty-one Geary could already look back on a distinguished career. Never once had he lost ground or stood still; always upward. As a soldier and an executive he had been honest, brave, and sincere, but most of all, he had been a man among men. Constantly in the van of American progress he had weathered the storms, "fought the good fight," and had come through triumphant.

His active months in California were spent in an atmosphere of danger and severe competition. That was no land for a weakling or one of unstable determination; it demanded courage, firmness of resolve, and a winning personality. Since Geary was blessed with all of these qualities, he took the lead and stayed there.

V

GOVERNOR OF KANSAS

GEARY, now reëstablished in western Pennsylvania, gave himself over to the quiet pursuit of agriculture and the raising of stock. This was an occupation which he had long anticipated, and now he was firmly resolved to spend the remainder of his life in work so congenial to his present frame of mind. His resolution could not even be shaken by an offer of the governship of Utah by Pierce in 1855. He was definitely out of public life —so he thought.

While thus pursuing the "even tenor of his way," he was once again called upon to be of service to his country. For in 1856 Pierce asked him to become governor of "bleeding Kansas," that turbulent land of factional dispute and sanguinary conflict.

It is fairly reasonable to assume that the Territory of Kansas would never have become a theatre of guerrilla warfare had the Missouri Compromise remained in force. By that act the land which constituted Kansas was to remain free territory. Yet in 1854 the trouble-making Kansas-Nebraska Act divided the land in question into two territories, Kansas and Nebraska. The energetic Douglas had been responsible for the division. This was a compromise measure, for if two territories were created, the South would have an opportunity to secure one for slavery. Since Nebraska had nearer access to northern immigration, it was conceded to the North. The South would then claim Kansas for slavery. Then, too, this arrangement would tend to keep the wavering balance of free and slave states fairly equal. The northern abolitionists, however, refused to concede this point. As a result, northern immigration poured into the territory, greatly encouraged by the ever active emigrant aid societies. Hundreds of antislavery men entered the territory with the express purpose of settling there. With these came bands of militantly violent abolitionists to insure the state against slavery. Of this latter group, and most famous of them all, was John

Brown, that fanatical but truly sincere man whose terrifying raids did nothing to assuage the situation, which with the passage of each day became more and more bitter.

To counteract this movement, those of proslavery feeling also urged settlers who were "sound on the goose" to enter Kansas. From across the Missouri border came swarms of resolute men who descended upon the territory with the single purpose of driving out or exterminating those who opposed slavery in Kansas. The situation was tense, a veritable dynamite depot attacked by incendiaries. The inevitable explosion immediately occurred, and the ensuing conflict involved repercussions that hurried the states into tragic fratricidal strife.

Of course the Democratic Administration looked upon Kansas troubles with grave concern. Newspapers the country over featured magnified tales of atrocious cruelties which inflamed the public mind. Stump orators harangued and demagogues foresaw dire calamities. The inevitable theological prognostications thundered warnings of a God grown tired of the indecisive tactics so prevalent at Washington. Unfortunately all the governors who were hurried off to the seat of trouble proved woefully inadequate. Reeder was appointed only to be recalled a few months later. Shannon, who replaced him, was equally short-lived. He fled from Kansas in fear of his life.

Something had to be done, and soon, or the chances of a Democratic return to power at the next election would be small indeed. A man was needed, a strong man, who would be able to restore order in Kansas and help to save the Administration's face.

In his frantic search for a suitable governor, Pierce hit upon Colonel Geary, whose reputation for executive ability, force of character, and integrity of will were well known. Here was a man who in a crisis had the unyielding qualities of a rock. This had been amply demonstrated on the Gold Coast as well as on the battlefields of Mexico. But would he accept? Would he assume the terrific responsibilities of a man who would enter seething Kansas as governor?

The Colonel did not want a political appointment. He was perfectly content with private life; but, after considerable persuasion, he was finally prevailed upon to tackle the arduous job. His country needed him; the party needed him—reasons enough. He was a firm believer in the inviolability of the Union and in the Democratic party. Evidences of his faith in the party are shown in a letter he wrote to Buchanan on the latter's nomination for the Presidency in 1856. He writes:

The Democratic party, which I believe, in the Providence of God, is destined to perpetuate our glorious Union, and our civil and religious liberties, may well congratulate itself on its signal good fortune in having accomplished your nomination.

Later on he had occasion to modify his faith in the party, and particularly in Buchanan.

Geary's acceptance of the appointment was hardly actuated by personal ambition. No one envied the large responsibilities of a Kansas governor, and at best the task was sure to be a thankless one—and so it developed. It is not too much to say that Geary went to Kansas because he thought that he was doing right and would be in a position to render an important service, and because he was promised entire governmental support in all his efforts to restore peace where chaos now reigned. Without this guarantee of the Administration's backing, it is inconceivable that he would have seriously considered the governorship, even for a moment. On this score he was soon to experience his greatest disillusionment.

After receiving the appointment in the last days of July 1856, he went to Washington to see William L. Marcy, the secretary of state, and receive his instructions, the gist of which was fairly simple: *Peace had to be restored in Kansas.* More particularly speaking, however, the instructions were: "To maintain the public peace, and to bring to punishment all acts of violence or disorder by whomever perpetrated and on whatever pretext."

These orders were broad enough to suit almost any executive and, elaborated upon a little more fully, they might have read thus: "Maintain the public peace" with the aid of the United States troops, and punish all those guilty of "acts of violence or disorder" with the aid of the United States courts, previously established. Simple enough, yes, but oh, so difficult to execute!

So, armed with a firm confidence in the Administration, a strong determination to succeed, and his adequate "instructions," the new Governor set out for Kansas to take over his executive duties. He reached Jefferson City, Missouri, on September 5, and on the following day had a long consultation with Governor Sterling Price.[1] The need for such a conference was evident as well as urgent. For some time steamboats on their way up the Missouri River had been halted and all the passengers of abolitionist sentiment forcibly removed. The condition of affairs was indeed deplorable, and Price agreed to bring such outrages to an end. He was as good as his word. From that time on, no steamboat passengers met with interference on their way to Kansas.

Little information concerning Kansas affairs was obtained from Price. He had heard a rumor that Lane was about to invade Missouri with a force of three thousand men. But he placed so little reliance on the report that he paid no attention to the entreaties of some parties to call out the military of the state.

At the termination of his conference, Geary boarded the packet *Keystone* and departed for Fort Leavenworth. On the way he met Shannon, the retiring governor, who was hurrying with all speed eastward. Into Geary's ears he poured a wild story of affairs in Kansas. Several threats had been made on his life, and he was still fearful of their being carried out. Kansas was a theatre of violence and slaughter. No one was safe there; corpses lay scattered about, and the smoke of burning buildings clouded the skies. In later years Shannon had exclaimed: "Govern the Kansas of 1855 and '56—you might as well have attempted to govern the devil in hell."

---

[1] Price was an influential Democrat and a proslavery leader who later played a conspicuous rôle in the Civil War. He always said that the idea of the Kansas-Nebraska Act of 1854 originated with him.

This was quite an introduction to the new Governor's scene of activity. He was nothing daunted, however, for it was no more than he had expected. He pushed on, soon to be precipitated into the whirling vortex of riotous and bleeding Kansas.

The party arrived at Fort Leavenworth on September 9, where Geary was received by General Persifor Smith, an old brother in arms during the Mexican War.[1] The General was in command of the United States troops in Kansas, but by reason of ill health (this ill health continuing throughout Geary's administration), his activities had been sorely restricted. The troops were there, ready for use, but the Federal Government's policy with respect to their employment had been loose and indeterminate.

At Fort Leavenworth Geary despatched a letter to Marcy in which he reveals an intention to disband a portion of the soldiers then in service (territorial soldiers called by Woodson, not the United States troops) and enroll "bona fide inhabitants as emergencies may require." This plan, as will be shown, he soon executed.

The United States district attorney, A. J. Isaacks, was also visited by the Governor, and urged to organize the judicial system more efficiently, to hold more trials, and to punish the true offenders. Isaacks had been lax in the performance of his duties, and in his interview with Geary showed little indication of being otherwise in the future. This was only the beginning of Geary's trouble with the territorial judges.

The Governor's trip from Fort Leavenworth to Lecompton, the capital of the territory, revealed to him a state of widespread desolation and suffering. He wrote a vivid account of his impressions as follows:

I reached Kansas and entered upon the discharge of my official duties in the most gloomy hour of her history. Desola-

[1] General Smith began his military career in Louisiana, where he raised a regiment for the Seminole War. Distinguished service in the Mexican War raised his rank from that of colonel to brevet major-general. His career in Kansas began when he was assigned military command of the Western Department in 1856.

tion and ruin reigned on every hand; homes and firesides were deserted; the smoke of burning dwellings darkened the atmosphere; women and children, driven from their habitations, wandered over the prairies and among the woodlands, or sought refuge and protection even among the Indian tribes. The highways were infested with numerous predatory bands, and the towns were fortified and garrisoned by armies of conflicting partisans, each excited almost to a frenzy, and determined upon mutual extermination. Such was, without exaggeration, the condition of the Territory at the period of my arrival.

On September 9, in a letter to Marcy, Geary reveals another phase of the picture in a letter to the secretary of state. He described Kansas as being overrun by armed ruffians of a transient character, who were there only to do mischief, and for no other purpose. Speaking of the Southern faction he said:

. . . the actual pro-slavery settlers of the Territory are generally as well disposed persons as are to be found in most communities. But there are among them a few troublesome agitators, chiefly from distant districts, who labor assiduously to keep up the prevailing excitement.

In speaking of their opponents he remarked:

It is also true, that among the free-soil residents are many peaceable and useful citizens, and if uninfluenced by aspiring demagogues would commit no unlawful act. But many of these, too, have been rendered turbulent by officious meddlers from abroad. The chief of these is Lane, now encamped and fortified at Lawrence, with a force, it is said, of fifteen hundred men.

When the party arrived at Lecompton, that dilapidated looking collection of shacks and saloons, the Governor issued an address in which he outlined the course he would pursue. His appointment, as previously stated, he had not sought. Nevertheless he now made clear that he would do his best to establish order where only violence and bloodshed reigned. The speech was carefully worded and logically arranged. It is evident that he desired to avoid all possibilities of misinterpretation. The act of Congress regulating Kansas affairs was dwelt upon at length:

A careful and dispassionate examination of our organic act will satisfy any reasonable person that its provisions are eminently just and beneficial. If this act has been distorted to unworthy purposes, it is not the fault of its provisions. The great leading feature of that act is the right therein conferred upon the actual and bona fide inhabitants of this territory "in the exercise of self-government, to determine for themselves what shall be their own domestic institutions, subject only to the constitution and the laws duly enacted by Congress under it." The people, accustomed to self-government in the states from whence they came, and having removed to this territory with the bona fide intention of making it their future residence, were supposed to be capable of creating their own municipal government, and to be the best judges of their own local necessities and institutions. This is what is termed "popular sovereignty." By this phrase we simply mean the right of the majority of the people of the several states and territories, being qualified electors, to regulate their own domestic concerns, and to make their own municipal laws. Thus understood, this doctrine underlies the whole system of republican government. It is the great right of self-government, for the establishment of which our ancestors, in the stormy days of the revolution, pledged "their lives, their fortunes, and their sacred honor."

Continuing, he declared that the frightful conditions existing in Kansas had to be remedied, and that the continued conflict and turmoil resulted only in harm and suffering to the citizens. But their salvation was in their own hands, and with utmost earnestness and sincerity he asked, "Will you not suspend fratricidal strife? Will you not cease to regard each other as enemies, and look upon one another as the children of a common mother, and come and reason together?" Whereupon he stressed the point that salvation lay in mutual coöperation, not in constant bickering, jealousy, and strife. The people of Kansas should gather about the council board and banish all "outside influences." Their redemption could come only from the action of bona fide inhabitants in enacting laws, "upholding her government, maintaining peace, and laying the foundation for a future commonwealth."

When he said that all "outside influences" must be disregarded, he of course had no reference to the laws of the United States.

All the provisions of the Constitution of the United States must be sacredly observed—all acts of Congress, having reference to this territory must be unhesitatingly obeyed. . . . In my official action here, I will do justice at all hazards. Influenced by no other consideration than the welfare of the whole people of this territory, I desire to know no party, no section, no north, no south, no east, no west—nothing but Kansas and my country.

He concluded his speech with a stirring plea to forget the past bitterness and begin anew.

To the bitter partisans, both slavery and antislavery, the address promised little—no leanings toward special privilege could be discerned. From his remarks they gathered that no partiality to factions would be shown. And they were right, for when the new Governor declared equal justice to all, he meant it.

Simultaneously with his address Geary issued two proclamations which aimed at the large bands of soldiers imported into the territory, chiefly from Missouri, by Woodson, acting governor, before Geary's arrival. Woodson had been led to believe by the incendiary Sheriff Samuel Jones that the forces of Lane and other Northern leaders could be thwarted only by the use of counter forces, and those of a proslavery character. Jones's demand for additional armed men had come after a prisoner had been removed from his custody by a group of free-soil settlers. Whatever the motive, Woodson's precipitate action could hardly be termed judicious. In a proclamation issued by him he declared the territory "to be in a state of open insurrection and rebellion." Further on in the proclamation he called upon all law-abiding citizens of the territory to rally to the support of their country and its laws, commanding "all officers, civil and military, and all other citizens of the Territory to aid and assist by all means in their power, in putting down the insurrectionists."

On the face of the matter, it is extremely difficult to determine just what Woodson had hoped to accomplish by the issuance of his proclamation. If the country was in a state of insurrection, surely his call for indiscriminate bodies of armed men would only aggravate the situation. Just who the "insurrectionists" were his proclamation utterly failed to make clear. Both slave and antislave parties had been invited to punish the offenders, with the result that both parties had organized for mutual extermination. None of the forces had been mustered into the territorial militia in the regular manner; all were poorly organized and loosely disciplined. Woodson even had sent letters into other states, particularly Missouri, asking for armed forces.

Thus Kansas was now an armed camp. The situation was the most critical in her history. Lane, with armies of variously estimated numbers, seemed to be everywhere, fighting for the Northern cause. From Missouri came bands of resolute men under Atchison and Reid, determined to wipe out the "damned abolitionists." Many writers are of the opinion that Woodson deliberately provoked what he thought would be a violent and decisive struggle which would settle the issue. L. W. Spring, in his *Kansas*, expresses the belief that had Woodson been acting governor for another few days the complete conquest of Kansas would have been assured.

To stem the threatening tide Geary issued the proclamations to which reference has previously been made. In the first one he declared that the employment of militia was not authorized by his "instructions from the General Government, except upon requisition of the commander of the military department in which Kansas is embraced."

He further declared that an authorized force was at his command sufficient to execute the laws, and that the services of the volunteer militia already employed were no longer necessary. In conclusion he commanded "all bodies of men, combined, armed and equipped with munitions of war, without authority of the government, instantly to disband and quit the Territory . . ."

In his second proclamation Geary asks for soldiers:

I, John W. Geary, Governor of the Territory of Kansas, do issue this, my proclamation, ordering all free male citizens, qualified to bear arms, between the ages of eighteen and forty-five years, to enroll themselves, in accordance with the act to organize the militia of the territory, that they may be completely organized into companies, regiments, brigades, or divisions, and hold themselves in readiness, to be mustered by my order, into the service of the United States, upon requisition of the commander of the military department in which Kansas is embraced, for the suppression of all combinations to resist the laws, and for the maintenance of public order and civil government.

The difference in the two methods of militia enrolment used by Woodson and Geary is made clear in this second proclamation. Geary had been authorized to enroll troops upon "requisition of the commander of the military department in which Kansas is embraced," while Woodson had no such authority. Hence all bodies of men called into action by Woodson were unlawful.

Geary's address and proclamations did not please all the citizens. Radical, subversive elements found nothing therein to encourage further violence, and the two dominant parties, pro- and anti-slave, found no comforting overtures held out for their support. But the solid residents who were there for purposes of home-making and peaceful agriculture were gratified to hear the guarantee of impartiality which rang throughout the speech.

The reception accorded to Geary's official pronouncements by the *Squatter Sovereign*—a newspaper published in Atchison by John H. Stringfellow and Robert S. Kelly—was anything but flattering. The editorial column on September 16, 1856, derided the new Governor and his efforts in no uncertain terms. In referring to his proclamations, it says: "The whole tenor of the documents, to us breathes a desire to avoid offence to either party, while it holds out an imbecile and tardy promise of punishment to offenders." His policy of "disbanding and re-banding" the paper feels to be all wrong. The editorial's last paragraph very bluntly reveals the *Squatter Sovereign's* true *raison d'être* as it concludes in the following self-accusatory fashion:

But our own party may thank themselves for this state of affairs. With the means of extermination in their own hands, at the propitious moment for bringing them into play, our forces are found making a retrograde movement.

The bloodthirsty *Squatter Sovereign* did not mince words; a general slaughter of all opponents to slave extension was heartily advocated.

Now that Geary had entered the scene, promising impartial treatment and a cessation of hostilities, such firebrands as John H. Stringfellow and Robert S. Kelly, editors of the above paper, could only condemn and ridicule. This blast against the new Governor was his first baptism of fire—and the mildest. Listening to his inaugural address, Geary's opponents must have realized that this huge man with the penetrating gray eyes would fight for his convictions to the very last. What they wanted was another vacillating Woodson, what they got was this adamant Pennsylvanian who would not deviate an inch from what he considered the path of right and justice. It is little wonder that they began a campaign of vilification and slander that was unique, even in an age famous for unremitting political vituperation.

No man ever began a gubernatorial career under less auspicious circumstances than did Geary upon his arrival in Kansas. Practically all of Pierce's appointees were proslavery in sentiment and action. They of course wanted a governor of similar convictions, but when Geary arrived they were sure that Pierce had made a mistake, and the President did assuredly err if he wanted to make Kansas a slave state. The southern constituencies were doing their best to encourage slavery in Kansas, and Pierce realized that it behooved him to keep in their good graces, but he also realized that the Democratic party would lose considerable prestige if the tragedies then being enacted in Kansas continued.

Since the free-state settlers in the territory had been accustomed to seeing proslave presidential appointees enter Kansas, they adjudged Geary to be of the same type. Consequently they were at first suspicious and distrustful, even going so far as to doubt his authority. But his proclamations and repeated promise of impartial justice, backed by conclusive executive acts which corroborated his stated intentions, caused them to realize that he was honest and sincere in his efforts to restore peace. They were tired of bloodshed. Assuredly there were some abolitionists who militantly insisted on direct opposition with resort to arms, but many of these, too, began to side with Geary.

The proslavery party had fully expected a kindred spirit to receive the appointment. Their choice was John Calhoun, the surveyor-general of Kansas and Nebraska. Therefore, as soon as word was received that Geary would be their new governor, they immediately set to work to frustrate and embarrass him, even before his arrival. Atchison,[1] Stringfellow, Reid, Doniphan, and others, vociferous in their demands for a slave state, had published a document which covered Geary's path with thorns and augmented the public excitement. A portion of their trouble-making address follows:

Though we have full confidence in the integrity and fidelity of Mr. Woodson, now acting as governor, we know not at what moment his authority will be superseded. We cannot await the convenience in coming of our newly appointed governor. We cannot hazard a second edition of imbecility or corruption.

We must act at once and effectively. These traitors, assassins, and robbers must be punished; must now be taught a lesson they will remember.

The object of the above is obvious. All those who openly opposed slavery in Kansas were to be forcibly evicted or silenced before Geary could arrive. They came close to realizing their designs, perilously close, but fortunately the new Governor was able to frustrate them before the movement had gone beyond remedial measures.

Of course two parties were required to make a quarrel, and

[1] David Rice Atchison, an influential United States Senator, was elected president *pro tempore* of the Senate sixteen times. It has been said that "Atchison became President for one day, when the 4th of March, 1849, fell on Sunday and Zachary Taylor did not take the oath of office until the day following." *Dictionary of American Biography*, I, 402–403.

while we have been dwelling on the agitators of the proslavery party, it must not be inferred that the free-state men were without blame in keeping the water boiling. Fanatical John Brown had listened to the sentiments expressed at the Kansas Convention at Buffalo on July 9 and 10 with hearty approval. Gerrit Smith voiced the opinions of the radicals there when he shouted,

You are here looking to ballots when you should be looking to bayonets; counting up votes when you should be mustering armed, and none but armed, emigrants. . . . They [members of the convention] are here to save Kansas. . . . But I am here to promote the killing of American slavery.

After the convention John Brown went to Kansas, where he and his small party committed the atrocious murders at Dutch Henry's Crossing. His capture of Pate, and other subsequent deeds met with reprisals on the part of the proslavery group. Tidings of these conflicts flew to the North, where excitable mass meetings resulted in a greater antislave emigration than ever before. The oratorical Lane left Chicago and proceeded to Kansas with what was called "the Army of the North," a body tremendously overestimated in power and numbers. To meet Lane an army of proslavery men was organized in Missouri to settle the issue once and for all.

This outside interference in the affairs of Kansas caused most of the trouble. If the territory's residents had been left unmolested, had been permitted to settle their disputes by legislation and recourse to impartial judicial proceedings, the story would have been much different, and far less bitter. Little wonder, then, that Geary stressed a hearty disapproval of "outside influence" in his inaugural speech.

The Administration at Washington was just as heartily opposed to all meddling from abroad in Kansas affairs. When James W. Grimes, Governor of Iowa, protested to the President that former Iowans resident in Kansas were not being "protected by the United States officers in the enjoyment of their liberty and

property," and that the President was to blame for much of
the trouble, Marcy, who answered for Pierce, replied in terms
of severe rebuke and condemnation to the Governor's imputations. This was a stinging reprimand, not only to Grimes, but to
all outsiders who took it upon themselves to interfere in Kansas.
Marcy's letter so well illustrates the Administration's policy that
it will not be unprofitable to quote it at some length:

> The President is not disposed to except to the style of your
> address, when you say to him, "as the executive of Iowa I de-
> mand for her citizens in Kansas protection in the enjoyment of
> their property, their liberty, and their rights," but would suggest
> to your excellency that such language implies a right to enforce
> obedience and the power to compel it. Neither of these is in-
> trusted to your excellency, and the President therefore pardons
> to your zeal what could not be forgiven to your good breeding.
> It is not strange that a government with such limited powers
> as are conceded by the constitution of the United States and
> conferred by the constitution of Iowa upon you should over-
> estimate himself. The doctrine that the executive of Iowa can
> protect her citizens beyond her borders, or that he has any
> authority beyond the limits of his state is an absurdity.
> The President, believing that a little reflection will convince
> your excellency that your jurisdiction of the citizens of Iowa is
> confined to the limits of your own state, still feels solicitous lest
> your excellency become excited and attempt some Quixotic
> redress, for the real or fancied wrongs of citizens of Iowa in
> Kansas, and therefore invites your attention to this clause in
> the constitution: Article 1, section 10. "No state shall, without
> the consent of Congress, lay any duty of tonnage, keep troops
> or ships of war in time of peace, enter into any agreement or
> compact with another state or with a foreign power, or engage
> in war, unless actually invaded, or in such imminent danger as
> will not admit of delay.

With an admonition to refrain from any rash act, Marcy concludes his sharp letter.

This intolerable interference from abroad was bad enough,
but the indifference and actual hostility of the civil officers in
the territory was, if anything, worse. As previously stated, the

presidential appointees in Kansas were of proslavery sentiment. Threatened by a large Northern immigration, they felt that Kansas could not be admitted as a slave state unless that immigration was forcibly discouraged. Southern immigration was inconsequential compared to that of the North, where the Emigrant Aid Societies were working so strenuously. The issue was simple to them: keep the abolitionists out by any means.

With fellow officials committed to such a program, Geary's mediatory and peace-bringing measures struggled hard for existence when balked by a wall of indifference and actual protest, erected by the very men whom he rightfully expected to execute his plans.

He therefore took the first opportunity to lay the situation before President Pierce. On September 19 he wrote a letter to the Chief Executive in which he bitterly asserted that "there is not one of the territorial officers competent or willing to discharge the duties of the position to which he has been appointed." Because of their inefficiency "there is little reason to wonder at the wretched and deplorable condition to which the Territory has been reduced." He then particularizes: "Judge Burrell is a nonentity. He has not been in the Territory two months since his appointment twelve months ago." He justifiably asks that Burrell be removed. Judge Lecompte is also blamed when he would not try 113 prisoners in Lecompton. Instead he went to his home in Leavenworth, fifty miles away, where he expected the prisoners to be sent to suit his own convenience. "This of itself," Geary declares, "I consider sufficient to justify his removal, to say nothing of the imbecility and utter worthlessness he has manifested during the entire period he has been in office." The United States marshal, I. B. Donelson, was declared to be lacking in courage and energy. Furthermore, he was too old; Geary wanted a young man to fill the office. The attorney-general was violent, uncoöperative, and negligent, refusing to appear at Lecompton when Geary sent for him. Also, he was one of the chief advocates of force and armed resistance to antislavery agitation.

In regard to Secretary Woodson [he continues] I have no words sufficiently expressive to convey a proper idea of my condemnation of his destructive policy. His proclamation, calling for volunteer militia from Missouri and elsewhere out of the Territory, exhibits an utter lack of sound judgment, and came nigh proving far more disastrous to the country than all the events combined that have transpired since the days that the first colonists landed on our shores.

Speaking generally again, he says:

All the officers of the territorial government are partisans on the same side of the great local question in which all the existing difficulties have had their origin. . . . In a word, there is not an officer, high or low, in the territory, who is amenable to the Governor or to the people. . . . The greater portion of the evils which this territory has suffered must be attributed to the incompetency of the men who were placed here for its protection.

Strong words, these, when we consider that the appointments were made with Pierce's cognizance. "The king can do no wrong" was just a phrase to Geary. The appointments were made; they were bad; they should be rectified. This letter was typical of Geary. If he felt a mistake had been made, by inferior or superior, he was not long in making his opinions known. "Yes men" no doubt flourished in that day as well as in this, but if one were desired in the executive chair of Kansas he could not be found in the closing months of 1856.

The general view of the Kansas situation previously presented has been set down to show just what obstacles confronted the new Governor as he took office. Beyond a doubt they were considerable. Yet, without fear or favor, he set to work to unravel this almost hopeless snarl of bitterness and strife. Let us now turn to a narration of the actual events which occurred as he attempted to put his discordant house in order.

The situation in Kansas was now one of the most critical in her entire history. An army of revengeful Missourians under Reid and Atchison was on her soil to exterminate, if need be, the free-soil exponents, while Lane was there with his army to prevent it. War to the death was imminent—unless it could be stopped.

Since the greatest trouble was expected at the town of Lawrence, occasional headquarters of Lane and his men, Geary kept a watchful eye upon that place by sending there a confidential agent, Theodore Adams, to report immediately any acts of violence or signs of approaching hostilities. On September 12 Adams informed his chief that a large force of men, three hundred of whom he had personally seen, was encamped six miles away.

Geary immediately notified Colonel Cooke of the United States forces at Lecompton, and they with three hundred men set out for Lawrence at 2:30 in the morning of the thirteenth. Upon arrival at the town they discovered everything to be quiet, but the citizens they found there were heavily armed, waiting for an expected attack from the Missourians. After looking over the situation in person, Geary addressed a public meeting in which he advised against any unlawful acts, promising them sufficient protection in case of attack.

Deeming a further continuance of his stay there unnecessary, and hearing that his presence was required at the territorial capital, he left for Lecompton. He was there only a few hours, however, when he again received an urgent dispatch from Adams, who reported that General Reid was in command of the invading army numbering about 2,700 men.

I saw and was introduced to General Atchison, Colonel Titus, Sheriff Jones, General Richardson and others. . . . The outposts of both parties were fighting about an hour before sunset. Secretary Woodson [who had been sent by Geary to disband the approaching force] thought you had better *come* with the militia on to the camp as soon as you can.

Upon receipt of this urgent summons Geary, accompanied by Cooke, again set out for Lawrence with three hundred soldiers and a battery of light artillery. When he reached the town his worst fears were confirmed. For he found the large invading force of almost three thousand men who, according to the

Executive Minutes, were "well armed and accoutred with all the customary munitions of war embracing a number of cannon. These were the Territorial militia. They were highly excited, and so eager and impatient for an assault upon Lawrence that it was with difficulty they could be restrained."

A desperate situation indeed faced Geary on that ominous evening of September 14 as he entered the town of Lawrence. Here he found every man, woman, and child capable of bearing arms standing ready to meet the attack which was expected any moment. Geary was firmly resolved that the anticipated attack should never occur.

Early on the following morning he went out to meet the invading army. As he went through the lines, already drawn up for battle, he heard dire prophecies and threats of assassination directed against him if he dared to prevent the attack on Lawrence. Fearlessly he strode through the mass of scowling men to confer with their officers. In simple and direct terms they were told that the attack must not be made, that it was unlawful and would be resisted by him and the United States troops to the utmost. Such an act would be a crime not only against Kansas, but against the United States as well, with the strong probability of a general civil war as a consequence. He concluded his speech by referring to his proclamations, and ordering an immediate dispersal of the invading army in the name of the President of the United States.

Fortunately the officers saw the wisdom and common sense in his words, and decided to accede to his demands. Some were reluctant to do so, but the majority acquiesced and gave orders for the abandonment of their plan.

In the meantime Lane, who wisely refrained from making an appearance at Lawrence, was reported near the Nebraska border, attempting to organize a larger army. In reality, upon hearing of Geary's disbandment proclamation, he had abandoned a project for the destruction of a group of proslavery men at Hardteville, known as Hickory Point. Before Geary's proclamations had been brought to his attention he had sent word for reinforcements from Lawrence. In answer to his summons, Colonel Harvey had left Lawrence with a band of free-soil agitators. The Colonel had not yet reached Hickory Point when he met a messenger from Lane who reported that the intended assault had been given up. Although Harvey was ordered to return to Lawrence, he disregarded instructions by attacking the defenders at Hickory Point. In the noisy battle that lasted for about six hours, several men on both sides were wounded and one proslavery man killed. When Geary was notified of the battle, he sent Colonel Cooke to stop it. Cooke arrested 101 of Harvey's men and brought them to Lecompton. After several delays the prisoners received a trial in October. Some were acquitted, but many were convicted of manslaughter and sentenced to from five to ten years at hard labor under ball and chain. Geary remitted the latter part of the sentence. As there was no prison, the men were placed in an old house under loose guard where practically all escaped. Those who did not escape were pardoned by the Governor.

These prompt and decisive acts of Geary's had succeeded in relieving the grave tension that had held the people of Kansas in its grasp for the past months. It must have been with a great deal of relief that he wrote Marcy on September 22:

Since the 16th instant, when I last addressed you, the affairs of the Territory have assumed a more peaceful aspect. . . . The principal and perhaps only difficulties that have since occurred, have been occasioned by strolling bands of marauders.

In the above-quoted letter Geary made three valuable suggestions for the improvement of Kansas: The opening of a land office was imperative, as the people continually quarreled over contested deeds and titles; a special mail agent was needed to stop theft of letters and packages; and a territorial prison was an immediate necessity.

On September 30, Geary again wrote to Marcy. This time he joyfully announces that "peace now reigns in Kansas. Confidence is gradually being restored. Citizens are returning to their claims."

The Secretary must have been amazed indeed to read those comforting lines. Unhappy Kansas, made chaotic by pillage, murder, and arson, was now quiet. The tempest had been replaced by a welcome calm.

Although actual wholesale bloodshed had ceased, and the greatest peril removed, Geary still had a number of troublesome fights on his hands. One of these had to do with his continued efforts to remedy the deplorably ineffectual judicial system. The latter had miserably failed in all respects, and the Governor felt that if the regularly constituted courts remained futile he would have to resort to martial law, a thing he was extremely loath to do. The judges appointed by the national administration were undoubtedly to blame for most of the miscarriages of justice in the Territory. Judge Cato was obviously of proslavery sentiment, for not only did he constantly associate with the ringleaders of that party, but he was also seen by Geary in the ranks of the Missourians at Lawrence. Chief Justice Lecompte was negligent, as will be shown, and Judge Burrell was not even in Kansas, as Geary complained in a previously quoted letter to Pierce.

In order to determine the reason for the poor reputation of Kansas courts, Geary sent a form letter to Cato and Lecompte. We shall quote the one addressed to Lecompte:

Executive Department, K.T.
September 23, 1856.

To the Hon. SAMUEL D. LECOMPTE,
  Chief Justice of the Supreme Court of Kansas Territory.

Sir: Upon my arrival here I found this territory in a state of insurrection, business paralyzed, operation of the courts suspended, and the civil administration of the government inoperative and seemingly useless.

Much complaint has been made to me against the territorial officers, for alleged neglect of duty, party bias, and criminal complicity with a state of affairs which resulted in a contempt of all authority.

I have therefore deemed it proper to address circulars to territorial officers, in order that, being informed of the complaints against them, they may have an opportunity to vindicate themselves through my department.

The efficiency of the executive will be much impaired or strengthened by the manner in which his subordinates in office discharge their respective duties.

As it is my sworn duty to see that the laws are faithfully executed, I need offer no apology for requesting categorical answers to the following interrogatories:

1st. When did you assume the discharge of the duties of your judicial office?

2nd. What counties compose your judicial district, and how frequently have you held courts in each county or in your district?

3rd. How many bills have been presented—how many ignored in your courts—how many indictments have been tried before you, and how many convictions had, and for what offences?

With a brief statement of other facts and circumstances, showing the manner in which you have discharged your duties, which you may be pleased to communicate.

Very truly, your obedt. servt.,
JNO. W. GEARY,
Governor of Kansas Territory

From the replies received by Geary, it seems that Cato had been in the territory for a year, having jurisdiction over eight counties. In that time he had tried one case for murder and two for assault with intent to kill. The murder trial and one assault case resulted in an acquittal, while the other resulted in a mistrial.

Lecompte had been in Kansas two years, with judicial authority over Atchison, Leavenworth, Doniphan, Jefferson, Calhoun, and Douglas counties. In answer to the question regarding the number of convictions in his court, he says:

The only convictions I remember are, one for horse-stealing in Doniphan, and some three or four for assuming office; one for maliciously killing a horse in Atchison county; one in Jefferson county for selling liquor to Indians; and perhaps some eight or ten in different counties for selling liquor without license.

Here was an amazing situation indeed. In a country where murder, arson, and rape were common, where lawlessness was the rule rather than the exception, the two judges in the most tempestuous part of the Territory could report no convictions of crimes more serious than horse-stealing, unlawful assumption of office, and the illegal sale of liquor. If one were to depend on these judicial reports for a true picture of the situation in Kansas, he would consider it a blissfully quiet land indeed.

The Hays case is an instance of Lecompte's carelessness in his official duties. After Geary had succeeded in disbanding the Missouri army on September 15, a band of riders, self-styled the "Kickapoo Rangers," on their way from Lawrence to Lecompton committed several acts of theft and molestation on the residents along the road. One resident, David C. Buffum by name, was shot in the abdomen while protesting the theft of his horse. Although Buffum, a cripple, was unarmed and practically helpless, his assailant shot him at close range with a pistol. Geary, accompanied by Judge Cato and others, happened along just in time to see Buffum die. Horrified, Geary promised to leave no stone unturned in an effort to discover the murderer.

Upon arrival at Lecompton, he issued a general warrant for the arrest of the murderer, as yet unnamed. It is curious to note that of all the arrests and detentions made on this warrant, not one was a proslavery man.

On the twenty-ninth, his efforts having been so far unavailing, Geary issued a proclamation offering a reward of five hundred dollars for information leading to the arrest and conviction of the man who had so wantonly shot Buffum.

Finally, information being received in the early part of November that a certain Charles Hays was the murderer, a new warrant was promptly issued, and Hays arrested. He was then brought to Lecompton where a grand jury, composed of proslavery men, found a true bill against him. He was committed for trial on the charge of murder in the first degree.

This pleased Geary, who was becoming more and more annoyed at the repeated arrests of free-soilers who were thrown into prison by the judges without admission to bail. It is to be seen that Geary had real cause for satisfaction when he considered that Hays, a proslavery man, had been held by a proslavery jury.

On November 10 the Governor was listening to a delegation of free-state men who had arrived to complain against what they thought was one-sided justice. They claimed that proslavery men were favored in the courts because the judges were sympathetic toward the slavery cause. Geary was in the very act of answering their arguments by citing the arrest and confinement of Hays, when a man entered to announce that Judge Lecompte had admitted Hays to bail, furnished by Sheriff Samuel Jones. Geary was amazed and angry. This last act of Lecompte's convinced him of his exact position as Governor. He was alone, surrounded by rabid partisans who were supposed to serve the Federal Government in a neutral fashion.

The delegation of free-soil men were now indulging in the pleasure of a few "I told you so's" when Geary jumped to his feet and pronounced the act of Chief Justice Lecompte in discharging the accused murderer of Buffum, after the grand jury had found a bill of indictment against him for murder in the first degree, as a judicial outrage without precedent, and as highly discourteous to himself, as he had been chiefly responsible for the arrest of Hays. He thereupon commanded Marshal I. B. Donelson to "re-arrest the said Charles Hays, if he be found within the limits of this Territory."

The Marshal declined to execute the order, saying that he desired time to consider it. Geary then gave the order to Colonel H. T. Titus, who immediately departed on his mission. Donelson had refused to obey the Governor, as he later declared in a letter, because he considered such action unlawful.

On the twelfth, Colonel Titus despatched a note to Geary saying that he had again arrested Hays, and was holding him subject to further orders. The prisoner remained in the custody of

Titus until Geary went to Leavenworth City to attend a public sale of Delaware lands. During his absence Hays was again discharged by Lecompte on a writ of habeas corpus, as Titus informed Geary in a letter dated November 21.

Geary did not contest the writ of habeas corpus, but he did send his executive minutes to Pierce, outlining the whole affair. Thereupon Pierce nominated Mr. G. O. Harrison, of Kentucky, to take Lecompte's place. But the Senate refused to confirm Harrison because the President had not issued a writ of supersedeas. Consequently Lecompte stayed in office. He had been removed along with Clark and Donelson, and Geary wrote Pierce that the removal "had been received here with general acclamations by the people, and men recently disposed to vilify and abuse you, are loud in your praise." He was yet to learn of the Senate's non-confirming action.

Continued trouble and petty annoyances from the judiciary were to bother Geary for the duration of his term.

After the Hays case, Lecompte sent a letter to Washington in explanation of his conduct which widely differed from some of the statements made about him by Geary in the letter to Pierce, quoted on page 72. Thereupon Marcy sent Geary a note demanding an explanation for the differences existing between the two reports. These differences could not have concerned the Hays case, because Geary's letter was written on September 19, only four days after the murder had been committed, and long before the matter was brought to Lecompte. They must have related to Geary's general condemnation of Lecompte.

In reply to Marcy's demand for an explanation, Geary laconically stated:

What I have written, I have written, and I have nothing further to add, alter, or amend on the subject. My executive minutes, faithfully chronicling my official actions, and the policy which dictated them at the time they occurred, and my various dispatches to the government, contain but the simple truth, told without fear, favor, or affection, and I will esteem it a favor to have them all published for the inspection of the country. . . .

Thus a new note begins to creep into the letters passed between Geary and Marcy. Geary now becomes terse and abrupt; but this should not occasion any particular surprise. Of all the communications received by Geary and placed in the executive minutes (at least those seen by the author), not one congratulates or thanks him for his efforts in restoring peace; all were aloof and perfunctory, without the slightest expression of gratitude. Now the Secretary hints of mendacity in his correspondent's statements. Geary's reply of the twentieth shows that he was then beginning to see what later became so obvious, namely, that the Administration was using him as a tool in Kansas that the Democratic party might again come into power. That being accomplished, Geary's policy of impartial justice could be replaced by something else—slavery in Kansas.

In speaking of Geary's trouble with Lecompte, Dr. Charles Robinson, in his *Kansas Conflict*, says that it was "soon discovered that Lecompte was the favorite at Washington, and not Geary, and that the effort to fasten slavery upon Kansas had been by no means abandoned. Geary eventually learned that he was mere surplusage, and only nominally Governor of the Territory."

Whether Geary really thought as this last statement claims he did is a matter for conjecture, but we must remember that Robinson, named by the free-state men as governor of Kansas, knew Geary personally, and discussed Kansas affairs with him often. But we must also remember that Robinson, as leader of the free-staters, bucking what he maintained was a proslavery national administration, when speaking of that administration would hardly tinge his remarks with admiration.

By the middle of October Geary's peace policy directed against the sanguinary war in Kansas had succeeded so well that he decided to make a trip over the Territory to get a first-hand view. His journey, lasting from October 17 to November 6, gave him opportunity to address numerous bodies of citizens and get their opinions. On his return he addressed a letter to Marcy in which he says:

The general peace of the Territory remains unimpaired; confidence is being gradually restored; business is resuming its ordinary channels; citizens are preparing for winter; and there is a readiness among the good people of all parties to sustain my administration.

Circumstances, generally speaking, looked pretty favorable for the Governor. Lane had definitely quit the territory, and Geary now notified General Persifor Smith that he could dispense with all United States troops except one squadron of dragoons and one company of infantry. Most of the soldiers mustered in pursuance to the demands of Geary's proclamations were paid and discharged at Fort Leavenworth. The Governor was now resolved to use the militia only in case of the direst necessity.

December passed off quietly, Geary spending most of his time within the executive "mansion," a single-storied shack conspicuous for its scarcity of windows. Typical of hasty pioneering construction, it presented a bleak appearance indeed.

On December 22 the Governor disclosed in a letter to Marcy several schemes used by the Democrats in Kansas to enroll him on the side of slavery. Tempting baits were offered, such as the governorship of Kansas after its admission to the Union, or a senatorship. In spite of these offers Geary would not deviate an inch from his declared policy. He thus describes these efforts made to enlist him on the side of partisanship:

Because I will not co-operate with certain efforts to establish a state government, and lend myself to carry out views which are outside of the Constitution and the laws, I am misrepresented by a few ultra men of one party. Because I will not enter upon a crusade in support of one idea, and endorse a series of resolves passed on the night of the last session of the Kansas Legislature, making but a *single issue* in Kansas, to wit the introduction of slavery; denouncing the national Democratic party from which I have the honor to hold my appointment; and branding as abolitionists or disunionists all persons not agreeing with these principles,—I am equally the subject of misrepresentation by a few violent men on the other side. My uniform reply to all objectors is, that my position shall not be prostituted to advance partisan ends, it being my simple duty to administer the government, and leave the people free to settle and regulate their own affairs.

The territorial officers, with scarcely an exception, were warm partisans of the last named party organization; so much so as to deprive themselves of all ability to act as mediators between the contending factions.

A legislature which would declare that a single issue existed in Kansas and that issue slavery, would undoubtedly prove intractable when working in conjunction with an executive who was pledged to impartial justice. So it proved when the Legislature did meet in January.

Yet it was not this Legislature which first occupied his attention, but another one, the so-called Topeka Legislature of anti-slavery sentiment which also claimed the power to make laws for the territory. This body came into existence as a protest to an election held under Governor Reeder on March 30, 1855. The free-staters claimed that the Legislature elected at that time had been chosen chiefly by the votes of men residing in Missouri who had come into Kansas only to cast a ballot for pro-slavery candidates. Thousands voted in this way. When the expected wave of protest went up, a congressional committee, after reviewing the situation, reported as follows:

By an organized movement, companies of men were arranged in regular parties, and sent into every council district of the territory and into every representative district but one. The numbers were so distributed as to control the election in each district. They went to vote, and with the avowed intention to make Kansas a slave state. They were generally armed and equipped, carried with them their own provision and tents, and so marched into the Territory.

Regardless of the number coming into the territory from Missouri, and the manner in which the election was held, the results are illuminating. Every member of the Legislature, excepting one (who later resigned), favored making Kansas a slave state.

So, contending that the Legislature had been fraudulently elected, the free-state men defiantly elected a legislature of their own. They also made a state constitution, known as the Topeka Constitution, which barred slavery from Kansas. Dr. Charles Robinson was triumphantly elected governor.

Consequently two governments existed in Kansas, one for each contending party. The free-state Legislature met at Topeka on March 1, 1856, and organized a state government. As a result of this action, Robinson and others had been arrested for high treason, but were subsequently released when it was learned that General James Lane was marching with a large army to free them.

Geary had long been looking forward to the meeting of this free-state Legislature, which was to convene at Topeka on January 6. Apprehensive of the results of this gathering, he had done all in his power to guard against any unlawful occurrences. This free-state body was illegal, and the Governor had left no stone unturned in an effort to prevent its successful meeting. In a letter to Pierce he outlined his precautionary measures taken to prevent an open conflict between the free-state legislators and the proslavery men:

I had confidential agents at Topeka and other places, and had every assurance that no quorum would be present and that no business would be transacted in the slightest manner conflicting with the territorial government. Dr. Charles Robinson gave me assurances that he would resign his Governorship, which he accordingly did, and he was on his way to Boston upon the day of meeting. W. G. Roberts, the Lieutenant Governor, I was informed, would not attend and Mr. Klotz, the Secretary of State was in Pennsylvania. So you will perceive that I had little occasion for apprehension.

To provide against all contingencies I had a reliable agent at Topeka to give me early notice of all movements, determining to repair there in case my presence became necessary.

The proslavery party in Kansas was also determined that the free-state Legislature should not meet. Their method of prevention, however, was a little more drastic than the Governor's, and one that might have resulted in a renewal of open physical conflict. "Certain officious gentlemen," declared Geary in the latter part of the above quoted letter, "in an attempt to cause trouble, sent the ex-sheriff Samuel J. Jones who made information against 34 members of the old Topeka Legislature for usurpation of office on March 4, 1856." Judge Cato issued a warrant to Donelson, who sent deputy Pardee *alone* to Topeka, where he "arrested twelve persons without the slightest resistance and brought them to Tecumseh, where waiving all examination they were held to bail in their own recognizance in the sum of Five Hundred Dollars each."

Geary was pleased when these men submitted peacefully and thus averted a disturbance. He said that the meeting at Topeka would not have been noticed except for the *faux pas* of the proslavery agitators. In fact the free-state prisoners, after being released on bail by Judge Cato, were never brought to trial, the district attorney entering nolle prosequi.

Why had the free-state men submitted so quietly to arrest? It can be attributed, no doubt, to the fact that they were disorganized by Geary's influence. No quorum could be obtained to conduct business. Also their leader, Robinson, had resigned as governor and was not in the territory. Roberts, the lieutenant-governor, was supposed to have presented Robinson's resignation to the Legislature, but he too was not in attendance. This temporary demoralization was all for the best; it saved Kansas a lot of bloodshed. Robinson was theoretically still governor, though from the viewpoint of the free-state supporters his resignation had not been presented to the Legislature. And when a convention was held later, on March 10, 1857, he explained why he had resigned. The members of the convention then requested and received a withdrawal of the resignation.

Two legislatures thus existed, both de jure in the eyes of their constituents, but only one of them lawfully existed; that was the first one elected (the slavery-favoring body), because it had been chosen under the provisions of the Organic Act with congressional authority.

Now that the illegal body had been dispersed (January 6, 1857), Geary was ready to turn his attention to the Legislative Assembly, convened at Lecompton on January 12, while the thermometer registered a temperature of thirty degrees below zero. The very composition of this Legislature rendered it hostile to the Governor: it was partisan, he was neutral; therefore conflict was inevitable. The battle was opened with the reading of his first message to the shivering but determined lawmakers.

Geary's communication began by summarizing the events that had transpired in Kansas since his arrival. Then he said:

Pledged to do "equal and exact justice" in my executive capacity, I am inclined to throw the veil of oblivion over the errors and outrages antecedent to my arrival, except so far as reference to them may be necessary for substantial justice, and to explain and develop the policy which has shed the benign influence of peace upon Kansas, and which, if responded to by the Legislature in a spirit of kindness and conciliation, will contribute much to soothe those feelings of bitterness and contention which, in the past, brought upon us such untold evils.

Still speaking generally, he enumerated the principles that would govern his actions and the issues to which he was committed. They were, he said,

Equal and exact justice to all men, of what ever political or religious persuasion; peace, comity, and friendship with neighboring States and Territories, with a sacred regard for state rights, and reverential respect for the integrity and perpetuity of the Union; a reverence for the Federal Constitution as the concentrated wisdom of the fathers of the republic, and the very ark of our political safety; the cultivation of a pure and energetic nationality, and the development of an excellent and intensely vital patriotism; a jealous regard for the elective franchise, and the entire security and sanctity of the ballot-box; a firm determination to adhere to the doctrines of self-government and popular sovereignty as guaranteed by the organic law; unqualified submission to the will of the majority; the election of all officers by the people themselves; the supremacy of the civil over the military; free and safe immigration from every quarter of the country; the fostering care of agriculture, manufactures,

mechanic arts, and all works of internal improvement; the liberal and free education of all the children of the Territory;
entire religious freedom; a free press, free speech, and the peaceable right to assemble and discuss all questions of public interest.

Referring to legislation, he exhorted them to enact no laws
which would not clearly bear the constitutional test;

. . . and if any laws have been passed which do not come up to
this standard, it is your solemn duty to sweep them from the
statute book.

The Territorial government should abstain from the exercise
of authority not clearly delegated to it, and should permit all
doubtful questions to remain in abeyance until the formation
of a state constitution.

Slavery should be subject to the decision of the courts upon
all points arising during our present infant condition.

Here he made it known that he would not favor slavery legislation, preferring to defer it to some other time. As it turned out
though, almost every important piece of legislation hinged
directly or indirectly on that explosive question. He expressed
the hope that all laws not appearing favorably when held up
to the light of the general and fundamental principles of government would be "revised, amended, or repealed." And in referring to the matter of inconsistent legislation, he said:

By carefully comparing the organic act as printed in the
statutes, with a certified copy of the same from the Department
of State, important discrepancies, omissions and additions will
be discovered. I therefore recommend the appointment of a
committee to compare the printed statutes with the original
rolls on file in the Secretary's office, to ascertain whether the
same liberty has been taken with the act under which they were
made.

Continuing in this vein the Governor then proceeded to
mention a fault in the Kansas Statutes: "Chapter 149, permitting
settlers to hold 320 acres of land is in violation of the preemption
laws, and lends to contention and litigation." He then criticized
the Legislature for usurping power. "There is not a single officer

in the Territory amenable to the people or to the Governor," he said, "all having been appointed by the Legislature, and holding their offices until 1857. This system of depriving the people of the just exercise of their rights cannot be too strongly condemned."

Concerning Indian lands, the Governor expressed the view that the red men had too much, more than they could properly handle. He would, therefore, be pleased to unite with the Legislature in any measure deemed advisable, looking to the speedy extinguishment of the Indian title to all surplus land lying in this Territory, so as to throw it open for settlement and improvement. The amalgamation of the American with any "inferior race," such as the Indian, he considered unwise and harmful. He thereupon suggested that certain general improvements should be made: boundary lines for all counties should be clearly established; the matter of damages incurred during the recent hostilities had already been referred to the Federal Government; the Kansas River should be made navigable as far as Fort Riley; and a geological survey should be undertaken.

This message to the Legislature has been dwelt upon at some length, for it gives a fairly concise view of the government in Kansas at this period. Showing a comprehensive grasp of the needs and deficiencies of Kansas, it not only criticized and blamed where blame was due, but it also carried a number of truly constructive recommendations. Glaring ills, many of them attributable to misbehavior on the part of the Legislature, existed, and the Governor did not spare the rod. The members had made mistakes, but it was never too late to mend. Undoubtedly there must have been some squirming and not a little anger on their part as they listened to the reading. Those of a vindictive nature were soon to get even by presenting all the thousands of little petty annoyances to the Executive, at which recalcitrant legislatures are so adept.

Trouble arose from the very beginning. The first move of the Legislature was to pass an act, the whole idea underlying which was directly opposed by the Governor. It provided as follows:

Section 1. The District court, or any judge thereof, in vacation, shall have power and authority to admit to bail any prisoner on charge, or under indictment for any crime or offense, or any character whatever, whether such crime or offense shall have been heretofore bailable or not; such court or judge, on every such application for bail, exercising a sound discretion in the premises. This act to take effect from and after its passage.

Geary immediately vetoed the bill on the grounds that such a measure would make it easy for the most notorious criminal to escape punishment; "that it would tamper with and corrupt the judiciary; that it would incite to anarchy and lynch law; that every man conscious of the uncertainty of punishment by the courts, will take the law into his own hands."

This bill opposed the very thing for which Geary had been fighting, proper trial and punishment of offenders. He remembered with bitterness the Hays case, as well as many others, and he knew that the future would only bring a repetition of such shameful incidents.

The Governor's veto meant nothing to the Legislature, for it immediately passed the bill over his head, according to a preconceived plan.

The next quarrel arose over the Sherrard case. William T. Sherrard had been appointed sheriff by a county tribunal, but when he went to Geary for official confirmation he was told that the correct blanks for such purposes were not immediately available, and his legal confirmation would have to be delayed until their arrival.[1] Before the blanks came, however, Geary heard so many bad reports concerning Sherrard's character that he was dubious about signing the commission. Then, after members of the county board who had made the appointment visited him, requesting that Sherrard's commission be withheld until they could hold another meeting and revoke the appointment, Geary was firmly resolved to refuse Sherrard's confirmation.

When the legislators heard about the incident they sent a

[1] Sherrard, a member of a respectable Virginia family, came to Kansas to assist the cause of slavery. His intemperate habits and violent disposition led him into many quarrels and disturbances.

letter to Geary demanding to know why he refused to commission Sherrard. Geary replied that the matter did not concern the Legislature, but was "a subject of inquiry only from the territorial courts."

Sherrard, angry at his failure to be made sheriff, vented his spleen by assaulting two members of Geary's household, his private secretary and John A. W. Jones. He also declared that he would attack Geary on the first opportunity.

The opportunity came one day when Geary visited the House, accompanied by John H. Gihon, his private secretary, and Richard McAllister. As he was departing, Sherrard, who had been waiting at the door, went up to him and shouted, "You have treated me, sir, like a damned scoundrel!" He was armed with two pistols and a murderous-looking knife, waiting for an opportunity to use them. Geary now made a decision which undoubtedly saved his life: instead of striking his tormentor or even tarrying to talk, he turned his back and walked away. Frustrated in his attempt, Sherrard now spit in the direction of the Governor, grasping a pistol in his hand, trying to get the courage to fire. Geary kept on walking. There was nothing else he could do, for neither he nor his companions were armed.

The House of Representatives showed its true nature and hostility to the Governor when it protested against a resolution condemnatory to the outrage. In justice to the Council, however, let it be said that that body passed a vote of censure against Sherrard's unwarranted assault.

The affair caused a great commotion throughout the territory. Many indignation meetings were held, and many resolutions passed denouncing Sherrard, as well as the House, for virtually endorsing his act. At a meeting held on Capitol Hill in Lecompton on February 14, a committee of Geary's staunch supporters read a report which criticized the assault on the Governor and expressed unqualified approbation of all his official acts. It concluded in part as follows:

Resolved, that we hereby tender Governor Geary, the people's friend, our earnest sympathy in the discharge of his responsible duties, and we pledge him the support of all the actual bona fide settlers of Kansas, without distinction of party . . ."

The report was signed by James H. Legate, James G. Bailey and W. Esley Garret, committeemen.

Many proslavery men in the crowd were opposed to any such action, and a riot immediately ensued. Sherrard, who was there to break up the meeting, delivered himself of some insulting remarks. When they were challenged by a Mr. Sheppard, Sherrard began firing. Sheppard tried to return the shots, but his percussion caps were wet and his revolver was consequently made useless. In the mêlée that followed he was hit four times, when a shot by an unknown person struck Sherrard between the eyes, entering his brain. This ended the fight, for the disturbing element had lost its leader.

Along with the annoyances created by Sherrard and the firebrand utterances of Clarke, Surveyor-General Calhoun, and Sheriff Jones, the hostile Legislature culminated its brief session by passing a bill, the injustice of which could be seen by any impartial observer. Known as the Census Bill, the new act provided for the taking of a census preliminary to an election to be held in June 1857, for delegates to a constitutional convention. Providing a franchise restriction, namely, that no citizen should be allowed to vote unless he had been in the territory prior to March 15, the bill prevented the exercise of suffrage of all those emigrants who would come into Kansas in the spring. But worse than this, the bill contained a grave omission: it had no clause providing for a general ratification of the finished constitution by the whole people before its presentation to Congress. This serious error, notwithstanding other important structural faults, would necessarily condemn the bill to certain gubernatorial disapproval. Even while the bill was before the committee for consideration, Geary had warned its proponents that a failure to provide for a popular ratification or rejection of the constitution would doom the act to his veto. Ignoring this preliminary objection, the bill was passed, and when the Governor's veto message promptly appeared, no one was surprised. Neither was anyone surprised when the Legislature almost unanimously passed it over Geary's head.

That the bill was unfair and unwise is shown by its subsequent history. Robert J. Walker, the governor who followed Geary, protested against it.[1] So did John W. Denver, acting governor during Walker's absence in Washington. And when the slavery-tinged constitution arrived in Washington without popular ratification by the Kansans, Buchanan went back on his pledges of support to Walker by rushing it to Congress. All this in spite of the fact that in Walker's inaugural address in Kansas he had made the following statement:

My instructions from the president, through the secretary of state, under date of the 30th of March last, sustain the regular legislature of the territory in assembling a convention to form a constitution; and they express the opinion of the president that when such a constitution shall be submitted to the people of the territory, they must be protected in the exercise of their right of voting for or against that instrument; and the fair expression of the popular will must not be interrupted by fraud or violence.

What Walker said concerning the ratification of the constitution promised justice to all citizens of Kansas, but when he attempted to put the words into action, Buchanan deserted him.

Having brought the Lecompton Constitution up to the point where it was introduced into Congress—and defeated through the efforts of Senator Stephen A. Douglas of Illinois—let us now turn to the troubles confronting Geary during the last few weeks of his stay in the Territory. The Sherrard incident, as well as others of a less serious nature, kept the citizens of not only Lecompton but the entire territory in suspense. Sheriff Samuel Jones, L. A. McLean, John Calhoun (not to be confused with John C. Calhoun), B. F. Stringfellow, and other agitators

---

[1] Walker, a citizen of Mississippi, came to Kansas with a fine political record. He had served in the United States Senate and as Secretary of Treasury under Polk. Not desiring the Governorship of Kansas, Walker had nevertheless been prevailed upon by Buchanan, an old friend, to accept the post.

kept the pot boiling in an attempt to create more excitement and further embarrass Geary's administration. Surveyor-General Calhoun, who had an immense patronage to bestow, believed that the Kansas statutes were not "instituted for the punishment of pro-slavery men." A man who would make such a statement would hardly favor impartial government. The above group was tireless in its efforts to frustrate Geary at every turn. It organized a party, known as the "National Democracy of Kansas," solely for the promotion of slavery. As a bait to induce Geary's participation in the party they offered him a senatorship, but when he indignantly refused they renewed their previous efforts to have him removed, even sending a delegation to Washington for that purpose.

With his ear close to the ground, the Governor was extremely sensitive to all the currents of unrest which were every day growing stronger and stronger. He wrote Buchanan on February 21 that peace in Kansas was decidedly precarious because of a few who held important positions. "As it is," he warned, "the utmost vigilance is necessary to guard against their evil machinations, which if not circumvented at every point, may yet lead to consequences far more deplorable than any that have yet occurred." He said that the executive, whoever he might be, must have the steady support of the General Government or "a renewal of disturbances, the extent and dreadful effect of which no man can foresee, is inevitable." In the latter part of this letter he made clear that if the men then in Kansas were to be kept in office by the Government, "my usefulness here must be materially diminished, and the sooner I am relieved the better will I be satisfied." This could not have been any plainer. For Geary was just about at the rope's end, and unless Buchanan would give him some assurance that new and impartial officials would be appointed for the territory he would abandon the office.

He ends his communication to Buchanan by requesting new territorial officers and a sufficient force of United States troops to maintain the peace.

Only a few days after sending the above letter, Geary sent

another one (March 4) which carried his resignation. What could have caused this seemingly abrupt decision to resign as governor of Kansas, and that on the very day which saw Buchanan, the object of his petition, ascend to the Presidency?

The disclosure of a few facts will immediately dispel any mystery surrounding his action, and likewise any doubt as to his justification for it. The reader will certainly wonder why he should ask that United States troops be stationed in Kansas when this account has made repeated mention of the presence of those troops, particularly at Lawrence during the first few days of Geary's term. True, federal troops were in Kansas, but Geary had had positive and unpleasant assurance from their commander, General Persifor Smith, that they would be removed. In this connection let us quote from two letters which passed between General Smith and Geary relative to the management of the United States troops in Kansas.

On February 9, 1857, during the Sherrard trouble, Geary wrote to General Smith as follows: "I require . . . two additional companies of dragoons, to report to me with the least possible delay. I think this is absolutely necessary, and I trust you will immediately comply with my request."

Instead of acceding to the Governor's wishes, General Smith refused to send troops, deeming such action unnecessary. Furthermore, he stated that "all the forces here have just been designated by the secretary of war, and are under orders, for other service more distant; and even the companies near you will have to be recalled."

Observe that when Geary had asked for the soldiers he had said: "I think this is *absolutely necessary* [italics mine], and I trust that you will immediately comply with my request." Instead of complying, Smith had promptly refused. The Chief Executive, on whose shoulders rested the peace of the territory, had asked for help from an officer of the United States army and had been refused, and that refusal had been prompted by an action of the Secretary of War, Jefferson Davis.

It must be remembered also that Geary had been sent into the strife-torn land expressly instructed by the President of the United States "to maintain the public peace" in the Territory of Kansas. Now in the official exercise of his duties, in an effort to maintain that peace, he was balked, as we have seen, by the very Government that commanded him. Torn between doubt and misgivings, he knew not which way to turn. But one thing he was beginning to understand: in a crisis he could not depend on support from Washington—and without it he was powerless.

Looking again at Geary's instructions, he was to punish "all acts of violence or disorder by whomever perpetrated." To do this it necessarily follows that he needed the helpful coöperation of a fair and honest judicial system. The foregoing pages of this work relative to the Kansas courts show anything but coöperative effort on their part; rather did they attempt to throw obstacles in Geary's way. And when the Governor requested the removal of such men as Cato and Lecompte, he was refused.

All the above having occurred in the administration of Pierce, did Geary have a justifiable right to expect any different treatment from Buchanan? This can be answered, and with proper reason, in the negative. First, all his letters to Buchanan, expressing best wishes for a successful term and asking instruction concerning Kansas affairs, had been totally ignored. Second, it would have been hard to find any good reason for believing that Buchanan's policy would have been any different from that exercised by Pierce, both being exceedingly sensitive to the wishes of the strong southern bloc of the Democratic party. Subsequent events proved this latter to be true when Buchanan's appointments in Kansas became known. All of them, Walker excepted, were firm believers in slavery. Finally, we must also remember how Buchanan failed to support Walker in *his* attempts at impartial justice in Kansas.

Yet, aside from purely political motives, Geary had another very good reason for resigning his position and leaving Kansas. The herculean duties devolving upon him ever since his advent into the territory, and the inhospitable shack in which he was forced to live, had weakened his strong constitution to such a degree that it was almost impossible for him to carry on. He had suffered several hemorrhages of the lungs, and was firmly convinced that unless he could receive proper care his life would "not be long," as he wrote Woodson, March 10, 1857.

During those last few weeks in Kansas the indomitable Geary had reached one of the lowest spiritual ebbs of his entire career. "My only consolation now," he wrote A. A. Lawrence, February 25, "is that my labors are properly appreciated by and that I have the sympathy of, very many of the best citizens of the Union."

In view of the facts above related there is little wonder that Geary sat down, on March 4, 1857, to write the following letter of resignation:

> *Executive Department, K.T.*
> *Lecompton, March 4, 1857.*
>
> *His Excellency, James Buchanan,*
> *President of the United States.*
> Dear Sir:— Please accept my resignation as Governor of Kansas Territory, to take effect on the 20th of the present month, by which time you will be enabled to select and appoint a proper successor.
> With high respect, your friend and obedient servant,
> Jno. W. Geary

With a heavy heart this staunch and rugged neutral, who had struggled for impartial justice in a land seething with fanatical partisanship, went to the post-office late at night and mailed his brief note. Intending to be circumspect in letting the news of his withdrawal become public knowledge, he took care that no other person in Kansas should know of it except his private secretary, whose honesty was unimpeachable. Yet early next morning every street corner and saloon saw men excitedly discussing the Governor's resignation. The postmaster had read it, as he had every letter or package addressed to or by Geary since he began his executive duties, and circulated it about the town.

On the tenth, Geary departed from Lecompton, leaving behind him the letter to Woodson previously referred to, in which he stated that he needed rest and wanted to "avoid so much conversation." When he added, farther on in the same letter, "I will be absent a few days from Lecompton," it would seem to imply that he intended to return. But return he never did. Woodson's next letter from him, dated March 12, was written on board a Missouri River steamboat: "As I am now absent from the Territory," he said, "the duties of the executive office agreeably to provision of the 'organic act,' will for the time being devolve upon you."

Geary was now definitely out of the territory, headed for Washington. After arriving there on March 21 he had interviews with Buchanan and several of the cabinet members. These interviews were his last formal acts having any relation to Kansas. Departing from Washington he left the hectic problems of his brief gubernatorial career behind him; all that remained were memories, many of them bitter.

VI

FIGHTING FOR THE UNION

AFTER his brief but hectic career in Kansas, Geary devoted his time to the pursuit of farming and a close study of the national and sectional disputes which were soon to cause America's greatest tragedy—the Civil War. Like an overloaded wagon the American system of government was straining and creaking along, pushed farther and farther into the mire by the ever increasing weight of the secessionist movement. Viciously sibilant cries of disunion and slavery spread over the land. Pamphlets and books, politicians and preachers scattered the seeds of unrest which were soon to grow into rank weeds of sanguinary conflict.

Although surrounded by strong beliefs and flying opinions, Geary was not at all undecided as to the course he would pursue should open warfare occur. Believing that the states should be permitted the exercise of a reasonable amount of self-government, he nevertheless held severely to the inviolability of the Union.

In a communication to Buchanan on the latter's election to the Presidency he said: "I know that your government will be a unit of Union men; that you will discourage all sectionalism, and ignore all men not fully known to yourself for their devotion to the Union, and whose patriotism is not above suspicion." To him it was inconceivable that the United States could ever be anything but one government, one people.

Concerning his views on slavery, we do not have anything in actual writing as definite as the above statement concerning national solidarity, but there are no positive facts attesting to his partiality for that institution. If we consider the influence and training of his mother, that kindly old lady who on the death of her husband had educated and manumitted several families of slaves, we must conclude that on the principles of liberty and justice he was opposed to any subjection of the human race, white or black. We must remember also that he had worked hard to have the free-state clause placed in California's state constitution. Nevertheless, in his administration in Kansas where the slavery question was paramount, his sense of fairness to both contending parties caused him to administer a strictly neutral government.

That the Colonel's professed love of the Union was not given in the spirit of lip service is amply shown by his response to the first guns in Charleston Harbor.

Geary drove in to a little village in Westmoreland County one morning and heard that his country's flag had been fired upon in the exchanges at Fort Sumter. He hesitated not a moment, for in less than an hour he had a recruiting office open. Hurrying back home he made immediate preparation to join the United States forces in the war. He made application to President Lincoln for the right to raise a regiment, and when the request was granted he hurried to Philadelphia and set up a camp at Oxford Park. Out of the sixty-six companies that offered to serve under him he selected fifteen. These were provided with uniforms and equipped at his own expense. On June 28 the Twenty-eighth Pennsylvania Regiment was mustered into the service of the United States, and on the same day Geary was appointed colonel of the regiment by Andrew G. Curtin, governor of Pennsylvania.

The regiment, composed of 1,551 men, was recruited from several counties: Luzerne, Westmoreland, Carbon, Cambria, Allegheny, and Huntingdon. For field and staff officers Geary had an efficient body of men: Gabriel de Korponay, lieutenant colonel; Hector Tyndale, major; John Flynn, adjutant; Benjamin Lee, quartermaster; Earnest Goodman, surgeon; Samuel Logan, assistant surgeon, and Charles W. Heisley, chaplain.

The regiment was presented with four steel guns by Charles Knap, of Pittsburgh, and from the many extra troops requesting admission to Geary's command he formed a regimental battery and named it for the donor of the guns. These pieces were later replaced by six ten-pounder Parrots, furnished by the Government.

In the meantime the military affairs of the Union were not flourishing. A woeful lack of military preparedness was painfully evident: the battle of Bull Run had been fought and lost, and a Confederate attack upon Washington was expected at any time. Maryland's allegiance to the Union was as yet undecided, and panic was in the air.

Although hardly yet ready for the field, Geary was ordered to report for duty, and on July 27 he moved forward with ten companies, the other five remaining at Philadelphia for further training under Major Tyndale.

Upon arrival at Nolan's Ferry the regiment was assigned to extensive guard duty over a territory embracing ferries, fords, mountain gaps, the Chesapeake and Ohio Canal, and the Baltimore and Ohio Railroad. They were also used to ferret out spies and rebel sympathizers who were keeping the Southerners across the Potomac informed as to Union movements and plans.

On October 16 Geary's command, while collecting forage supplies, met and repulsed a superior body of rebels under Generals Ashby and Evans. The battle was long drawn out and sharp, but the boys from Pennsylvania acquitted themselves nobly, driving the enemy from the field at all points. This was the first victory after the disaster at Bull Run. For his signal success Geary received the thanks of the President, the Secretary of War, and the commander, General Banks, under whom he was serving at the time.

During the winter months the Twenty-eighth Pennsylvania was very seldom idle. It built roads and bridges, foraged for supplies, and had numerous brushes with the enemy's skirmishers and advanced lines. One of the most prominent deeds of the regiment was to chase General A. P. Hill out of Leesburg. It was also instrumental in driving back four thousand of the enemy who attempted to go to Frederick in order to sustain the Maryland Legislature as it contemplated an ordinance of secession.

The frustration of this movement played a decisive part in keeping Maryland out of the Confederacy.

Not once had the regiment been defeated. As a reward for his admirable services, Geary was made a Brigadier General of Volunteers by the War Department on April 25. He was then assigned to a brigade in the Second Corps, and attached to McDowell's division. After the promotion Banks wrote:

I congratulate you on your late promotion, and regret only that your brigade is not to join us again. Our connection has been long, and to me most pleasant, and I shall be glad at all times to acknowledge the efficiency, alacrity and unsurpassed energy and ability with which you and your command have discharged *all* your duties.

His detachment from Banks was of brief duration, for on the seventeenth he was again placed under that general's command. During July he was put in the advance lines, having almost daily contacts with the enemy.

On August 9, General Pope ordered Banks to assume command of all forces in front, and if the enemy advanced, to attack immediately. At Cedar Mountain the enemy was met in force under the leadership of Jackson. Unfortunately Banks underestimated the force opposite him, and instead of playing safe, ordered an attack. Geary's brigade was in the center of the battle line, supported on the right by S. W. Crawford, and on the left by H. Prince and George S. Greene. G. H. Gordon's brigade was stationed in the rear as a reserve. When the battle commenced, Geary and Prince charged forward, striking the brigades of J. A. Early and A. G. Taliaferro. The Confederate lines, much surprised, at first gave way in confusion, with exception of Early's command which stood firm. Had Early retreated, the day would undoubtedly have been lost by the rebels, but as it was he stood long enough to allow A. P. Hill to bring up reserves which attacked Crawford's exhausted men. In the meantime, Lieutenant-Colonel T. S. Garnett and Taliaferro, who were rallying their troops in the rear, soon came forward again to attack the now battle-worn Northerners. The latter, having borne the brunt of battle, and being in no condition to meet fresh troops, soon gave way. Geary and C. C. Augur were both wounded; Prince had been captured. The superior numbers of the enemy now rolled over the Union troops, and the battle was finished.

Geary's wounds, one in the foot and one in the shoulder, were severe, necessitating his withdrawal from command. It was while he was convalescing that he heard the disheartening reports of Pope's disaster at the Second Battle of Bull Run.

Shortly after his return to active service Geary gave up his brigade, on October 1, 1862, and assumed command of the Second Division of the Twelfth Army Corps, which he organized. During the winter of '62 and '63 his command was very seldom idle, but no major battles were engaged in by him during those months.

A. E. Burnside had succeeded to the supreme command of the Army of the Potomac, but after his disaster at Fredericksburg he was removed in favor of "Fighting Joe" Hooker. It was under the command of Hooker that Geary engaged in the battle of Chancellorsville, on the second and third of May. The Twelfth Corps under H. W. Slocum fought heroically. Geary displayed his usual courage and resourcefulness. At eight o'clock on the second day of fighting, he received an order to vacate the breastworks which he was holding with W. S. Hancock. But knowing that his retirement would permit the enemy to cut the Union army in two, he refused to obey until the order was sent in writing. Consequently he stood firm, withstanding some of the bitterest attacks of the entire two days' engagement. Later it was ascertained that the order received by him was a mistake, and the records do not show who sent it.

While exposed to a terrific fire Geary was knocked unconscious by the force of a cannon ball which passed between him and his horse's head. As he fell to the ground, those near by thought he had been killed, for blood was oozing from his eyes, ears and nostrils. The force of the missile was tremendous. Many weeks passed before he could speak above a whisper.[1]

The Battle of Chancellorsville went against the Union arms, but Geary's "White Star Division," so designated before the fray, served in a noble and distinguished fashion. It next saw action in the famous battle at Gettysburg.

As Lee marched into Pennsylvania a cloud of gloom hung over the North. With his hitherto invincible army of seventy thousand it seemed that he could not be stopped. Hooker, in his efforts to thwart the rebel commander's designs, engaged in an altercation with H. W. Halleck over the disposition of ten thousand troops stationed at Maryland Heights. Because the troops were not placed under his command to halt Lee he, in a fit of anger, resigned as commander of the Army of the Potomac. His resignation was accepted, apparently with alacrity, and General George G. Meade, a man of scholarship and courage, was appointed in his stead. Determined to meet and fight the enemy, he followed Lee northward. As both armies gathered about the little town of Gettysburg, their commanders maneuvered for advantageous positions; each seemed eager for a fight.

When General J. F. Reynolds, commander of the First Corps, met the Confederate forces in the immediate vicinity of Gettysburg, he called for Howard to advance with the Eleventh. Thus he selected the battlefield and opened the Battle of Gettysburg.

The Second Division did not arrive at the scene of battle until the evening of July 1, but they were just in time to assist the hard-pressed Eleventh Division, which was fighting and retreating through Gettysburg. Geary spent the night in the vicinity of Little Round Top. On the next morning he was sent to Culp's Hill, where he immediately began to erect fortifications. Culp's Hill later proved to be a very important point in the fighting which immediately ensued. He held the hill during the day until late in the afternoon, when he was required to lead

[1] "Life and Services of John White Geary," p. 131. This manuscript is unpublished, and anonymous except for the signature "F." It is owned by Alfred H. Geary, Rosemont, Pa.

two brigades in another part of the field. While he was away a rebel force overran a portion of his fortifications. Geary immediately attacked, the struggle lasting until ten o'clock of the third day. Then with a last desperate assault he succeeded in driving the enemy from the field. When the fierce battle was over, twelve hundred Confederate dead lay on Culp's Hill, mute evidence attesting to the sanguinary nature of the conflict.

It was on this last day of fighting that Lee watched the handsome George Pickett make his gallant charge. It failed. Other desperate attempts to dislodge the Union soldiers from their positions also failed. Lee, after suffering terrific loss, decided to retreat, the day ending with victory for the Federal arms.

Meade again followed the Confederate General, this time out of Pennsylvania, and although Lincoln earnestly requested another battle the Union General did not bring it about. During the month of July the slowly moving Army of the Potomac trailed Lee southward. But as Lee, not yet ready for another engagement, continued his careful retreat, Geary's division, still a part of the Twelfth Corps, saw no severe action. Somewhat disappointed at the turn of events Geary, along with many other officers, believed that a golden opportunity to stamp out the rebellion was definitely lost, at least for the time being. After crossing the Potomac on pontoons at Harper's Ferry his command proceeded to the Rappahannock, where during the sweltering days of August the troops were occupied in guarding the fords of the river.

A little more than two months after the Union victory at Gettysburg came the doleful news of General William Starke Rosecrans' defeat at Chickamauga. After a fierce two days' struggle (September 19–20) with General Braxton Bragg, Rosecrans had been forced to retreat to Chattanooga, where his badly damaged army, facing starvation and annihilation, was tightly encircled by the victorious Confederates.

Obviously the situation was extremely critical, and reinforcements necessary, else the imprisoned army, now under the command of General George H. Thomas, would be destroyed.

Thomas, whose heroic behavior in the battle just ended had earned him the title "the Rock of Chickamauga," was courageous and resourceful, but his position was now hopeless.

Fortunately for Thomas help was soon forthcoming. On September 23 the Eleventh and Twelfth Corps were taken from the Army of the Potomac and placed under the command of General Hooker, who had instructions to rush to the aid of the beleaguered army at Chattanooga. The troops were hurried by rail to Washington, thence to Columbus, Indianapolis, Nashville, and finally Murfreesboro. The latter town was reached on October 5.

A few days after his arrival Geary went to Fosterville, about thirteen miles south of Murfreesboro on the Nashville and Chattanooga Railroad, where he directed the construction of a fort for the railroad's protection. But just when the fortification was nearing completion, orders were received to proceed to Bridgeport. Here Geary, accompanied by his brigade commanders, waited for the troops to gather. After their arrival the division crossed the Tennessee River and marched for Wauhatchie Junction, past the towering peak of Lookout Mountain.

Then General Grant also arrived upon the scene, and a plan was devised to free Thomas and open a road for supplies. In the movement along the base of Lookout Mountain Hooker had unfortunately left Geary isolated with about fifteen hundred men. This error was seen by the watchful Confederate officers on Lookout, and they instantly realized that if Geary could be annihilated the forces of Thomas would be left open to a direct attack from the rear. Accordingly on the night of October 27 a heavy force descended upon Geary's troops. That officer, however, was not caught entirely unawares, for he had realized the danger of his position and had hurriedly erected light fortifications. As an additional precaution he had thrown out unusually heavy picket lines. When the attack came, a little past midnight, these advance troops fought stubbornly, retreating slowly back to the main body which was given time to make ready for the onslaught.

There in the darkness a terrific struggle ensued. Time after time the fierce rebel attacks were repulsed with heavy loss. Although far superior in numbers, and surrounding their foes on three sides, they could not penetrate to the center of the camp. Only the incessant flashes of musketry and artillery lighted the scene, and as they fought hand-to-hand it was hard to tell friend from foe. Geary was everywhere, encouraging his soldiers, repelling attacks. Galled by the effective Union artillery, the Confederates directed a withering fire on the Union batteries, mowing down horses and men. Edward R. Geary, a lieutenant of artillery and son of the General, was shot through the head while sighting his gun. He died in his father's arms. For several hours the engagement continued in unabated fury. Finally, noticing uncertainty in the enemy's ranks, Geary ordered a wild attack which swept all before it. At the same time a band of mules stampeded out of camp directly at the enemy. Thinking it was a Union cavalry charge, the rebels fled. So ended the Battle of Wauhatchie, the outcome of which was so important in the Chattanooga campaign.

Samuel P. Bates, in his book *Martial Deeds of Pennsylvania*, pays a glowing tribute to Geary for his remarkable achievement at Wauhatchie:

When Generals Grant and Hooker arrived (later in the morning), and witnessed the evidences of the intensity of the struggle, they expressed their surprise and gratification that so small a body of men had made so gallant a fight. General Slocum wrote: "I wish your command to know that I feel deeply grateful for their gallant conduct, and for the new laurels they have brought to our corps." Badeau in his life of Grant says: "Mr. Jefferson Davis had visited Lookout Mountain only a week before, and feasted his eyes with the sight of the National army shut up among the hills, like an animal ready for slaughter; and now at a single stroke, the prey had been snatched from his grasp. The door for relief was opened, and, from a besieged and isolated army, the force in Chattanooga had suddenly become the assailant. . . . The army felt as if it had been miraculously relieved. Its spirit revived at once, the depression of Chickamauga was shaken off, and the unshackled giant stood erect." "For almost three hours," says General Hooker in his official report of this battle, "without assistance he (Geary) repelled the repeated attacks of vastly superior numbers, and in the end drove them ingloriously from the field. At one time they had enveloped him on three sides, under circumstances that would have dismayed any officer except one endowed with an iron will, and the most exalted courage. Such is the character of General Geary." No words could more veritably portray his character, and the victory achieved

'In the dead waste and middle of the night'

against numbers many fold his own acting upon a preconcerted and well-matured plan, was gained by that iron will and most exalted courage."

Although the Union forces around Chattanooga were now in better shape than they formerly had been, the Confederates still held the strategically important Lookout Mountain. From its lofty, almost impregnable heights, they could observe in every detail the Union movements. Also, while holding this unique position, they were enabled to endanger a road of supply and communication so necessary to the Federal troops. Undoubtedly they had to be removed, but how?

After the arrival of Sherman with his corps, Grant decided to engage the enemy in battle with the hope of driving them out of the region. As Lookout Mountain was deemed inaccessible at the time, it was planned to stage a demonstration there, without any intention of storming the heights. If the battle favored him Grant knew that it would then be possible to shut off all rebel communications, rendering the lofty Confederate stronghold untenable. Geary, hearing of the plans, and believing that the enemy could be more easily and quickly chased out of the valley if Lookout were first captured, requested that he be allowed to lead a detachment up the mountain for that purpose. Grant gave his permission, allowing Geary to use full discretionary powers in executing his difficult task.

Early on the morning of November 28, screened by a dense

fog, he worked his strong column, supported by Whittaker's brigade in reserve, to the very foot of the mountain. The Confederates were totally ignorant of his presence until the first sentry gave the alarm. Like an overwhelming tide Geary's veterans swarmed over the first lines of defense before his foes recovered from their surprise, and started up the mountain. As the sun blazed forth word of the attack spread from peak to peak. Every obstacle, natural and man-made, retarded their progress. The path was narrow at all places, defended by numerous sharpshooters who lay in wait. Climbing through treacherous gullies and crevices, over huge, perpendicular rocks they forged ahead, Geary in the lead. Every foot of the way was bitterly contested, but the blue tide could not be stemmed. Yelling exultantly they engaged in hand-to-hand combat, overcoming each well-laid line of defense. The fighting continued all morning and into the afternoon. The summit was reached and Geary was still advancing steadily when a heavy fog enveloped the peak. It was so dense that all fighting had to be suspended. Geary took advantage of the ensuing lull to send for more ammunition. The fog continued to lie like a pall over the waiting troops, but before the battle could be resumed what little daylight penetrated the dense mass disappeared as darkness came on. During the night an unusual stillness marked the enemy's lines, and Geary suspected that they might have evacuated their position. His suspicions were correct, for when the new day appeared, not a Confederate was in sight. Lookout Mountain was now in possession of the Union forces, and when Geary's battle flag waved from the summit its appearance was greeted by a roar of cheers from the waiting men below.

Geary's assault on Lookout Mountain had been the signal for fighting all along the line. The forces of Hooker, Sherman, Sheridan, and Thomas attacked the enemy on November 24, 25, and 26. The fighting was fierce, but the enemy was dislodged, the rebels now retreating into Georgia. Fortune had smiled exceedingly bright on the Union troops in the battles of Missionary

Ridge, Ringgold Gap, and Chattanooga. Rosencrans' besieged army had been saved by Grant, who was every day growing more and more popular in the North.

After the battle of Chattanooga many of the Federal troops remained in that vicinity in winter quarters, waiting for the coming of spring. Geary was there during the winter months also, with the exception of a few days spent in Philadelphia for the purpose of persuading several thousand discharged soldiers to renew their terms of enlistment. He returned to camp where Sherman was concocting his plans for a daring march through Georgia, the famous march which was to split the Confederacy in twain, and bring to the Union General everlasting renown.

His plans completed, Sherman left Chattanooga on May 6, 1864, with some ninety-nine thousand men. His adversary was General Joseph E. Johnston, who had a smaller force, but was favored by a knowledge of the country and an excellent system of fortifications. Geary's "White Star Division" was now listed under the Twentieth Corps.

Sherman's army fought almost one continuous battle during the entire march to Atlanta. Day after day they toiled forward, meeting the rebels everywhere. At Kenesaw Mountain Johnston made a stand which Sherman was unable to take by assault. After losing three thousand men in the attempt, he made a flank movement which succeeded in dislodging the foe.

The campaign to Atlanta ended with the bitter fight at Peach Tree Creek. Geary's division was in the midst of it, fighting desperately every inch of the way, and losing a large number of men.

After the battle thousands of shells were hurled into the doomed city. Stubborn resistance was made, but it was fighting for a hopeless cause. On September 2 it was evacuated, and the White Star Division led the way in.

Geary admirably summarizes the Hundred Days' campaign in his official report:

Thus gloriously ended the campaign, unequalled for brilliant victories over seemingly insurmountable difficulties, and unsurpassed in history—a campaign which will stand forever a monument to the valor, endurance and patriotism of the American soldier; four months of hard, constant labor, under the hot sun of a southern summer, scarce a day of which was passed out of the sound of the crash of musketry and roar of artillery; two hundred miles travelled through a country, in every mile of which nature seemed leagued for defense—mountains, rivers, lines of works—a campaign in which every march was a fight, in which battles followed in such rapid succession, and were so intimately connected by an unremitting series of skirmishes, that it may properly be regarded as one grand battle, which crowned with grander victory, attests the skill and patience of the hero who matured its plans and directed their execution.

Sherman's army remained in and around Atlanta until November 15. On that day the first column started for the city of Savannah, three hundred miles away. In this march, unlike the one from Chattanooga to Atlanta, the army had very little heavy fighting to do. Destruction being the aim, a swath of devastation miles wide was cut across Georgia. Hardee, the rebel commander, offered a show of resistance at Savannah, but it soon wilted under the energetic fire of the invaders.

The army had approached the outworks of Savannah on December 10, encamping about three miles from the city to erect temporary breastworks. It was on the twentieth of the same month that Geary, ever watchful, saw the enemy quietly evacuating the town. Hurrying forward with part of his command, he was met at two o'clock in the morning by the mayor and a delegation of the Board of Aldermen, who bore a flag of truce and formally surrendered the city to him. Geary's were the first troops to enter Savannah. Because of this vigilance and quickness to act, he was honored with the military governorship of Savannah. But when Sherman again took up his travels Geary was relieved of his post to take part in the march through the Carolinas.

This time Geary was commanding as a brevet major general, for on January 12, Lincoln had made him a major general, "for fitness to command and promptness to execute," as stated in the official appointment.

The campaign out of Savannah was much more arduous and difficult than was the trip from Atlanta. The region itself presented many obstacles, and the weather was severely inclement. Important bridges were contested, and severe skirmishes constantly occurred.

After leaving the city of Raleigh, Johnston and Sherman entered into negotiations five miles outside the present city of Durham, which resulted, on April 26, in the surrender of Johnston's army. Lee had already surrendered to Grant, and with the yielding of Generals Kirby and Smith, the rebellion was over.

Geary's division was then marched to Washington, by way of Richmond, and disbanded on July 18, 1865. The General now went to rejoin the members of his family at Harrisburg, Pennsylvania, where they had been living during his absence in the field.

VII

GOVERNOR OF PENNSYLVANIA

RETURNED now to civil life, Geary devoted his time for the next few months to strengthening his financial position which, naturally enough, had not prospered during the war. While in the field he had not lost touch with Pennsylvania politics and politicians, having been in correspondence with such an eminent man as John Covode, member of the House of Representatives from Pennsylvania. Later, Covode was to work strenuously to secure Geary's nomination for the governorship of Pennsylvania.

Political activity brought Geary into contact with Simon Cameron, that astute manipulator who had been Secretary of War under Lincoln and was later to become influential in the United States Senate. He had already started to organize a political machine that became unique in the history of Pennsylvania. Cameron had definitely decided to support Geary in the Republican convention which was to meet in the summer of 1866 to nominate a candidate for governor. Cameron's sponsorship of Geary assured the latter of special consideration because Cameron's weight was already making itself known. A. K. McClure, in his book, *Old Time Notes of Pennsylvania*, makes this clear when he says:

I was a delegate to the convention, as were Colonel Mann, Colonel Quay, Tom Marshall, Senator Finney, Senator Ketchum and a number of other active Curtin men, and we were greatly surprised to learn, when the convention met, that it was absolutely a Cameron assembly. He had, for the first time, won absolute mastery of the Republican State convention and the organization, and his candidate for Governor was General Geary, who was especially objectionable to the men I have named and many others, because within three months of the meeting of the convention, he had written a letter to Mr. Maguire that was given to the public, assenting to the use of his name as a Democratic candidate for the same office.

Cameron wanted the convention to give either a direct or quasi endorsement of the Johnson administration, but a minority of the nominating body headed by Colonel Quay warned Cameron that such a plan would split the party. Cameron acceded to the demand, believing, however, that the convention was unwise in its resolve to oppose Johnson.

McClure cites considerable opposition in the convention to Geary's nomination on the part of certain members who doubted his sincerity and fidelity. They felt that one who had so recently been an ardent Democrat was not to be trusted with the high office of governor of Pennsylvania. Yet, when the minority could present no candidate of their own, and when Cameron's real strength was manifested, Geary's nomination became a certainty. The Republican party in Pennsylvania would stand or fall with the doughty General.

After Geary's nomination Simon Cameron admirably reviewed the political situation in Pennsylvania from the Republican angle when he wrote, in August 1866, to his friend Charles A. Dana concerning his prospects of being elected to the United States Senate. He said:

Now as to the Senator. I don't see how the combination can defeat me, and yet I shall not be cosy till it's over. [The combination he referred to was the Curtin-Forney group.] Geary knows very little of the state, when he says that Forney can defeat me, who really cannot command any number of votes. . . . . Stevens if he were younger,—if he had more health, or if he was not considered almost absolutely necessary where he is, would run away with it—as he really deserves to, in consideration of his great abilities, and his constant devotion to the right —but quiet, sensible men may hesitate to elect a man who may die before his seat is ready, and who cannot live more than a year or two. . . . You will not believe me, and yet I would not begrudge the place to him. If he and I had been listened to at Balto [Baltimore] we would not be cursed with Johnson. Curtin will be the great competitor, and may be elected. His election would be a great misfortune to the country. . . . He made a speech last week for Geary and will speak for him till after the election, and as soon as it is over, will go to Washington swearing that he did it to hold Pennsylvania for Johnson. The original bargain was to elect republicans enough with the democrats in the Legislature to re-elect Cowan for which Curtin was to go to Italy—but seeing that Cowan can elect no republicans, their programs have been changed. You will see this is a strong combination—and yet if the map does not greatly change, I will whip them, and drive all its elements where they belong.

My great desire now is to elect Geary. I care for that much more than for the Senatorship—for the reason that in my opinion the safety of the country depends on the success of the Union party in Pennsylvania in October—and we will win.

With the above prophetic utterance Cameron concluded his letter.

Geary's nomination on the Republican ticket presents a question on which considerable light must now be thrown: When and why did he change party affiliations? From the moment of awakening political consciousness Geary had been a strong Democrat. All his political appointments had been from that party. It had his unqualified support in word and action, and he believed, as he wrote to Buchanan in 1856, that only on the principles underlying the party could this country's prosperity and greatness be perpetuated.

While governor of Kansas his treatment at the hands of the Democratic Administration had been rough and inconsiderate, yet his faith in the party remained steadfast. Undoubtedly he was annoyed at the preponderance of Southerners in Buchanan's cabinet, and at Buchanan's failure to support him. Yet he did not resign as governor because of slavery, but because he received no Administration support in his policy of impartial justice in Kansas. He was still a Democrat in 1856, and later he voted for Douglas in the next presidential election. Geary struggled through the Civil War, saw the slaves freed by a Republican President, and still remained a Democrat. And it was only three months before the Republican convention, as previously stated by McClure (see page 113), that he had given his permission, *by a letter which was made public*, to have his name used as a candidate for governor *by the Democratic party*. This evidence certainly seems to warrant the conclusion that Geary changed his party affiliation within a space of three months.

Evidence counter to the above exists in an interesting unpublished volume (to which reference has already been made) entitled "Life and Services of John White Geary," written by a personal friend. This author attributes his subject's shift in party loyalty to the slavery issue. He says that when Geary "found the Democratic party drifting under pro-slavery influence," he felt himself

alone and powerless for good. The issues of slavery, long dormant, [?] enabled him to work with the party; but now that it had come to the surface [in the Kansas conflict of 1856] and been espoused by the Democratic party, he could no longer array himself under that banner, without violating all the instincts and principles of his nature. Besides, he was intensely loyal, and could not be allied with any party that even remotely threatened the integrity of the Union. Such were his feelings during the political canvas that placed Mr. Lincoln in power. However, he supported Mr. Douglass, although he had hardly forgiven him his part in the repeal of the Missouri Compromise, which had opened the door to the prevailing agitation that was fast precipitating the country into civil war.

At length slavery bore its legitimate fruit of secession and open, defiant rebellion. On that day he renounced the Democratic party, because he felt that it had renounced the great principles that underlie the foundation of our government. He no longer took any part in politics—his life was engrossed in the field. He was rejoiced to see Mr. Douglass rally to the support of the Administration, but he freely declared his unalterable resolution to break all connection with the party.

The above quotation clearly declares that Geary broke with his party because of the slavery issue, and yet, standing out like a red light, there appears the information that *he supported Douglas in his campaign against Lincoln.* Surely, if slavery was not an issue in the minds of the American people at that time, it never was an issue.[1]

Assuming then that Geary bolted his party after the Civil War, what were his motives for such a step? The answer may perhaps be found in a speech made by him as a candidate for governor in the summer of 1866. "The Democratic party," he declared, "has abandoned its old truths. You cannot get one of them to sign his name to any of its old cardinal doctrines. All the old Democratic doctrines and all the grand old principles of that party have come out and gone into the Republican party." A man who believed that, as he did in 1866, would have ample reason to change his party affiliations.

Geary inaugurated his campaign for the governorship of Pennsylvania at Erie on September 12, 1866, as a member of the National Union, or Republican party. The issues were largely national, involving the treatment of the southern states and the acceptance of the Negro as a bona fide citizen. This was emphasized at Erie when the candidate informed a huge mass meeting "that the questions now at issue are comprised in the amendment to the Constitution, proposed by Congress as conditions precedent to the admission of the Southern States to their old relations with the General Government—relations interrupted by the war." He maintained that Negro suffrage was not a civil rights question, but was to be considered in the field of political rights, and under such an interpretation Negroes could never vote in Pennsylvania without an amendment to the state Constitution. Every man in the South should be equal, and no more than equal. That three-fifths of the Negroes should be represented by white people was decidedly unfair.[2] Such a ruling

---

[1] This obvious self-contradiction is an example of several other inaccuracies which appear in the work, chief of which is the statement that Geary's first wife was a Miss Black, and his second wife a Miss Lee (pp. 370–371). In reality, their names were, respectively, Miss Margaret Ann Logan and Mrs. Mary C. Henderson. The latter names were obtained from the late John W. Geary, Jr., son of Governor Geary.

[2] Here Geary was referring to the representation clause that was placed in the National Constitution as a compromise measure.

applied when Negroes were slaves, but times had changed—they were free now.

The candidate's audience at Erie heard President Andrew Johnson bitterly derided for attempting to bring back the South on the old terms. "We want the South to come back to its old relationship," the orator said, "but it must be on terms of perfect equality." Here it is made clear that the most decided difference between the Republican and Democratic platforms at this time was the interpretation of the Civil Rights Bill. The Democrats insisted that the bill declared the right to vote, while their opponents denied that such a construction could logically be made.

McClure sums up the situation in Pennsylvania as follows:

I regarded it as a most important political contest that was to settle, once for all, whether the logical fruits of the war for which so much blood and treasure had been given should be realized by the North. It is probable that the Republican Congress would have had the same conflict with Johnson if Pennsylvania had voted Democratic in 1866, but that struggle was the crucial test of the willingness of the loyal states of the North to accept a policy of reconstruction that restored to full authority in the rebellious states those who had battled to destroy the Union, and who, in their efforts at reconstruction, had made the condition of the emancipated slaves even worse than it was in the state of slavery.

Railway expansion in the state was also considered an issue of notable importance. It was on this subject that Geary was asked a critical question: "Will you, if elected Chief Magistrate of Pennsylvania, faithfully exert the power of your administration to defeat any and every attempt made by legislation or otherwise, for the monopoly and control, by one corporation, of the railroad policy of the State?" To this the candidate replied that he was not in favor of the creation of any monopoly in the railroad system of the State "which would place it above and beyond the reach of the Legislature."

Geary's Democratic opponent for governor was Heister Clymer, of Berks county. He was an able man, but his open approval of Johnson's reconstruction plan was decidedly unpopular. The Republican papers united as one voice in labeling him "copperhead" and "traitor." Out in Chicago General Ulysses S. Grant told the editor of the Chicago *Republican* that "to ask any soldier to vote for such a man [Heister Clymer], of at one time known disloyalty, against another who had served four years in the Union army with credit to himself and benefit to his country, was a gross insult."

As the vitriolic campaign whirled along, Geary's personal popularity rapidly increased. Aided by an admirable war record and a winning platform manner, he impressed his audiences favorably. Then, too, and not to be ignored, the subtle maneuverings of Simon Cameron played no mean part in swinging the balance in his candidate's favor.

The contest was decided on election day, October 9, and when all the ballots were counted Geary was credited with a majority of 17,178 over Clymer.

The successful campaigner, both in politics and war, was inaugurated governor of Pennsylvania at Harrisburg, on January 15, 1867. A huge procession in celebration of the event started at the Jones House, and after winding through a number of streets came to a stop in front of the Capitol where, at twelve o'clock noon, it heard Geary swear "to support the Constitution of the United States and the State of Pennsylvania, and to perform my official duties with fidelity."

Immediately after his inception into office the new Governor delivered an inaugural address which outlined the policies of the forthcoming administration. The first part of the speech showered unsparing censure on the instigators of the recent rebellion. "The object of the South," said the Governor, "was avowedly the dissolution of the Union and the establishment of a confederacy based upon 'the corner stone of human slavery.' To have submitted to this on our part, and to have shrunk from a manly resistance under such circumstances would have destroyed the value of the priceless legacy bequeathed to us by our fathers, and which we are obligated to transmit unimpaired to future generations."

At the end of his long discourse on reconstruction problems Geary expresses regret that the "General Government has not taken any steps to inflict the proper penalties of the Constitution and laws upon the leaders of those who rudely and ferociously invaded the ever-sacred soil of our state." The speaker dubbed the General Government's failure to punish severely the perpetrators of "the greatest crime 'known to the laws of civilized nations' as morbid clemency."

In speaking of education the Governor said that the foundations of democracy rest upon the public schools. Pennsylvania schools should equal in excellence those of the New England states, and should overcome such obvious shortcomings as brevity of terms, lack of proper schoolhouses, and the employment of unqualified instructors.

Turning to the subject of "home resources and home labor," Geary asserted that it was clearly

. . . the interest of the nation to foster and protect domestic industry by relieving from internal taxation every sort of labor, imposing such heavy duties upon all importations of foreign manufactured articles, as to prevent the possibility of competition from abroad. Not only should individual enterprise and industry be thus encouraged, but all public works, among these a liberal and properly restricted general railroad system, and internal improvements of every kind, should receive the fostering care and most liberal aid of the government.

When he came to a consideration of finances, he stated that

. . . taxation should be applied where its burdens may be least felt, and where it is most just that it should be borne. Every resource should be carefully husbanded, and the strictest economy practiced, so that the credit of the State could be maintained on a firm and enduring basis, and the debt surely and steadily diminished, until its final extinguishment. Unnecessary delay in this would, in his opinion, be incompatible with the true interests of the citizens.

The Governor concluded his address by again alluding to the national situation. He began this particular phase of his speech as follows: "We are confessedly in a transition state. It is marvelous how prejudice has perished in the furnace of war, and how, from the very ashes of old hatreds and old parties, the truth rises purified and triumphant." Then farther on he again touched on the "ashes of old hatreds" as he referred once more to the Southerners:

The violators of the most solemn obligations, the perpetrators of the most atrocious crimes in the annals of time, the murderers of our heroic soldiers on fields of battle, and in loathsome dungeons and barbarous prisons, they must not, shall not, re-appear in the council chambers of the nation to aid in its legislation, or control its destinies, unless it shall be on conditions which will preserve our institutions from their baleful purposes and influence, and secure republican forms of government, in their purity and vigor, in every section of the country.

Apparently some of those "ashes" were still a little warm—farther down in the heap.

During his first term Geary had occasion to stem the rising power of the railroads, particularly the Pennsylvania Railroad, that child of a government's benevolence which, growing mightily, was ever greedy for additional privileges. When "An Act to Repeal an Act to Authorize the Pennsylvania Railroad Company to Increase its Capital Stock to Issue Bonds and to Secure the Same by Mortgage" was presented, the Governor promptly vetoed it. But, lest his "opinion should be misconceived and misrepresented," he thought it due to himself

. . . to make a brief exposition of some of the enactments of the Legislature, for the benefit of the Pennsylvania railroad company, since the original act for its incorporation, approved April 13, 1846, so far as relates to its capital stock.

By the first section of the act of incorporation, the capital stock was fixed at $7,500,000.

The twentieth section is as follows: "that if any increase of the capital stock shall be deemed necessary, in order to complete or improve the said railroad or appurtenances, it shall be lawful for the stockholders of said company, at any annual meeting, or at any special meeting convened for that purpose, in manner as aforesaid, to increase and dispose of any additional number of shares, not exceeding fifty thousand, so that the whole amount of said capital stock shall not exceed ten millions of dollars, and receive and demand the moneys for additional shares, in like manner, subject to the same conditions hereinbefore provided for the original subscriptions, as shall be provided for in the by-laws of said company."

The manner prescribed for the increase and disposition of the stock, in the foregoing section, is certainly most unexceptionable. It being under the direction of the stockholders, and not at the option of the directors, as is provided in the bill under consideration, and which is deemed objectionable.

The twenty-second section imposed a tonnage tax as one of the conditions upon which the original charter was obtained, which has since been repealed by statute, and the accumulated tax released.

By act approved April 23, 1852, the capital stock was increased to $13,000,000; May 6, 1852, to $14,000,000; March 23, 1853, to $18,000,000; May 2, 1855, to $20,000,000, and March 2, 1866, to $30,000,000.

Protesting the greatest friendliness to both the railroads and the Legislature, Geary nevertheless decided that the act, in allowing the board of directors to increase its capital stock in unlimited quantities, was "contrary to the spirit and intention of our institutions." Dangerous power would be gained by the railroad, and such power, "in irresponsible hands, would be unlimited and uncontrollable by any power short of revolution."

The true source of power should reside in the hands of the stockholders, not the directors.

The Governor saw the bill as a monopoly creator, and if his campaign promises were to be fulfilled, all monopolies must be discouraged. In a preëlection speech he had stated that while the big corporations continued "to act their part, as public servants, they should be carefully protected. They should not be permitted to overstep their legitimate functions. As creatures of the law, they should obey, and be, in every respect, subservient to the law."

The Governor concluded the veto message by stating that the people of Pennsylvania were opposed to the granting of monopolies and, as their servant, he would support them.

The above message was written on March 20, 1867, and later, on the twenty-eighth of the same month, he disapproved of another railroad bill which provided that the bonds of the Colebrookdale Railroad Company "be exempt from all taxes, except State taxes, until the net receipts of said road shall be sufficient to pay yearly six per centum per annum upon the cost of construction." The Governor refused his signature on this bill because it exempted property from tax. "Taxation, to be just," he said, "should be uniform, and, so far as practicable, it should be made to bear alike upon all property in proportion to its value." However, he did not exactly mean *all* property, for previously he had approved certain acts exempting the holdings of religious and charitable institutions.

The Governor's annual message of January 7, 1868, advocated a general railroad law on the free principle, because he felt it would create new markets, increase property values, stimulate trade, and make for greater prosperity. It was also suggested that passenger and freight rates be reduced.

In March of the same year the Legislature passed a free railroad law similar to the one desired by Geary, with two exceptions. The bill authorized any group of persons, numbering not less than nine,

. . . to form a company for the construction of a railroad, giving to them corporate privileges, provided ten thousand dollars of stock for every mile of road proposed to be made is subscribed, and ten per centum paid thereon in cash. Companies created under the act [were] to have power to borrow money, not exceeding the amount of capital stock subscribed, and to issue bonds of the company thereof to an amount not exceeding double the amount of subscriptions actually paid in, at a rate of interest not exceeding 7%.

The Free Railroad Bill was refused the Governor's sanction because it was unconstitutional, having more than one subject, and also because it permitted the increase of capital stock without limit. The "increase of stock" clause was a good example of "rider" legislation.

On September 6, 1869, Pennsylvania was horrified at the news of the great Avondale mine disaster. One hundred and eight men at the Avondale mine were burned or suffocated to death when the shaft timbers became ignited, shutting off the sole avenue of escape to the miners in the pit below. In his annual message of January 5, 1870, the Governor deplored the "selfish and parsimonious" way in which the mines of Pennsylvania were managed. To lessen the danger to miners, he suggested safety legislation along the following lines: The sides of the shaft should be constructed of incombustible materials; fans, not furnaces, should be used to ventilate mines; and every mine should have "more than a single avenue of ingress and egress." That he was not at all backward in condemning carelessness and selfishness, even when it concerned a group as powerful as were the mine operators, is rendered obvious from the above remarks.

Aware of the huge number of pardons issued by his predecessors and the time required to consider such petitions, Geary, at the beginning of his term, issued a public statement outlining the procedure to be followed by those who wished to make application for pardons. Regulations concerning their issue were enumerated as follows:

First. "No pardon will be granted until notice of the application therefore shall have been given by publication once a week for two consecutive weeks in a newspaper printed in the county in which the conviction was had."

Second. "No pardon will be granted unless notice of the application shall have been given to the judge who tried the cause, to the district attorney who prosecuted; proof of which notice shall be furnished to this department."

Third. "All applications must have a certified copy of the whole record, a full statement of the reasons upon which the application is based." There must also be a "copy of commitment: petition from prisoner setting forth reasons, and a statement from warden and inspector of prison."

Fourth. "No personal application will be permitted."

Fifth. All papers must be printed in pamphlet form, twelve copies of which "must be sent to this department." A poor person was exempted from printing the pamphlet.

Even after this well-considered program was put into effect, state-wide clamors arose protesting against the excessive number of pardons issued. Geary was at a loss to understand this, for during the entire year of 1867 he had pardoned only fifty-two people, all on petty offenses—the lowest number of pardons issued since 1848. Then the mystery was suddenly dissipated. The Governor learned, much to his regret and anger, that the Philadelphia court of quarter sessions had been in the habit of remitting and changing sentences months after they had been issued. In his annual message of January 7, 1868, he declared that during the preceding year as many convicts had been liberated from the Moyamensing jail by the Philadelphia court of quarter sessions as had been pardoned by him from all the prisons in the commonwealth. That such a practice was vicious and without lawful sanction, he had little doubt. "If," he said, "a judge can remit or shorten a sentence, he can increase it, and that is a power dangerous to allow anyone to wield. And further, if it be lawful for the judge of one court to remit sentences at pleasure, it follows that judges of all other courts should be invested with the same prerogative; and it requires no argument to show to what a dangerous extent it might be used." However, the Governor was relieved to know that such evil practices had been confined to only one court.

When the judges in the offending court heard of Geary's rebuke, they accused him, in offensive and vindictive terms, of gross misstatement. Particularly obnoxious was the reply of Judge Allison, whose remarks were downright insulting.

The newspapers took up the quarrel, and many were the stinging editorials directed at the Philadelphia court. One paper justified the Governor's stand in the following statement:

The pardoning power must not rest with the authority which convicts. . . . Fatal would it be to our interests if the practice of the Philadelphia judges is to be enlarged, because with that enlargement will come a judicial tyranny, arrogant, aristocratic and destructive. The undignified conduct of a portion of the Philadelphia judges, and the coarse language in which they indulge are well worthy the serious consideration of the people. . . . . Surely such a spirit demands instant rebuke.

Since the judges obstinately refused to accede to Geary's demand, the case was brought to the Supreme Court of Pennsylvania by Attorney-General Benjamin Brewster, where the state's contentions were sustained. The court handed down an opinion which stated that "if a criminal is convicted, his sentence must be revised, if at all, during the term in which it is pronounced."

The subject of pardons continued to irk Geary throughout his first term. He again mentioned it in his annual message of January 5, 1870, this time with considerable irritation. Petitions for pardon had become so numerous that a mere examination of them consumed a large amount of valuable time. During the year 1869, 1,550 applications for pardon had been made, of which sixty-two, or four per cent, were granted. The Governor complained that public sentiment had become perverted on the subject of pardons. "The framers of our government, as I understand it," he said, "never contemplated an indiscriminate use of the pardoning power. It was only designed for the correction of manifest errors or oppressions. . . . Both the theory of our government and public policy require that the pardoning power should be kept within these reasonable limits; and not be made an instrument to defeat the execution of the laws and the administration of public justice."

The pardoning power was to become an issue in Geary's next campaign for governor.

VIII

SECOND TERM AS GOVERNOR

GEARY's first term as governor was only about two-thirds over when prophecies on the next election began to appear in the Pennsylvania press. As early as December 25, 1868, it was observed that the Republican ranks were a unit for his renomination as their candidate. The caption, "For Governor, Major General John W. Geary," began to head editorial columns with almost daily regularity, and according to the Venango *Citizen* nine-tenths of all the newspapers favored the present incumbent, although no moves had yet been made by the state committee.

The Republican State Convention met at Concert Hall, Philadelphia, on June 23, 1869, and nominated Geary for governor on the first ballot. The voting went as follows: Geary, 122; Lilly, 6; Meade, 4; Porter, 1. Cameron was still supporting Geary. That and the candidate's personal popularity clearly show that they had the Pennsylvania Republicans in the hollow of their hands at the convention.

The Democratic convention did not function so smoothly as its Republican predecessor. The two leading candidates were Asa Packer, the Lehigh Valley millionaire railroad magnate, and General George W. Cass. A few delegates favored General Hancock, but as the members gathered, a letter was received from Hancock in which he declined to have his name considered. Then the Cass men made a strong effort in behalf of their favorite candidate, but after a few preliminary demonstrations of the overpowering strength of Asa Packer, the latter was nominated by a large majority.

Packer had not sought the nomination, preferring to devote his time to the Lehigh Valley Railroad. And, according to McClure, he did not attempt anything like a thorough canvass of the state.

The campaign of 1869 lacked the sprightliness that had distinguished the one in 1867. This lack was largely due to the

decreased emphasis placed on national issues which had provoked such bitter controversy in 1866. During the electioneering
Geary stood on his record, declaring that during his term the
burden of taxation had been removed from the shoulders of the
common man and placed on the corporations who, because of
the special privileges they enjoyed, were "justly made to contribute to the government which protects them. Mr. Packer,"
said Geary in a speech at Bradford, referring to his opponent,
"would restore the tax on real estate." When he came to a
consideration of bad legislation and his attempts to curb it, the
Governor referred the electorate to his numerous vetoes:

My predecessor, during the six years of his administration,
wrote 114 vetoes—just 19 per annum. Of the three years of my
administration thus far, I have written . . . 217 vetoes, in which
I will venture to say, almost every principle of the government
has in some way been involved. And no one of these vetoes has
ever been overridden by the Legislature. . . . I have gone just
as far as any Governor ever dared to go. No Governor has ever
vetoed as many bills and stopped as much evil legislation.

The subject of pardons aroused considerable interest during
the campaign, and the Democrats based their attack on Geary
through this issue. They claimed that he had abused his power
by issuing too many pardons. There was little reason for such an
accusation, however, for according to a list of pardons issued
by thirteen preceding governors, Geary had handed out less
than any of them. The highest number of the thirteen was 1,909,
granted by Governor Thomas McKean. Andrew Curtin had
issued 900, while Geary had agreed to only 198 such petitions.

The Republican press attacked Packer's wealth, predicting
that his election would result in legislation for big business.

Election day, October 12, 1869, dawned wet and miserable,
and the vote throughout the state was light, because of almost
incessant rain. When all the ballots were counted, Geary received 290,552 to Packer's 285,956, giving the Governor a
majority of 4,566. The Republicans also obtained a majority in
the Legislature: twenty-five in the House, and five in the Senate.

The new administration was but freshly launched when the Legislature, yielding to the influence of a powerful railroad lobby, passed an objectionable bill under the following title:

An Act to Facilitate and Secure the Construction of an Additional Railway Connection Between the Waters of the Susquehanna and the Great Lakes, Canada and the Northwestern States, by Extending the Aid and Credit of Certain Corporations to the Jersey Shore, Pine Creek and Buffalo Railway Company, and in Like Manner to Aid the Construction of the Pittsburg, Virginia and Charleston Railway, the Clearfield and Buffalo Railway and the Erie and Allegheny Railway.

In order to "facilitate" the construction of the four roads mentioned, the bill provided that the $9,500,000 worth of bonds ($6,000,000 in bonds of the Pennsylvania Railroad Company, and $3,500,000 in the Allegheny line) held in the sinking fund be withdrawn and distributed to the four roads.

In a long veto message to the Senate, where the bill originated, Geary condemned the act in no uncertain terms. Clearly it was a glaring example of omnibus legislation, enacted by the log-rolling device, and as such was beyond the pale of the loosest possible construction of the State Constitution. In the first place, the constitution, in the twenty-fifth section of the first article, declared that "no law hereafter enacted shall create, renew or extend the charter of more than one corporation." This bill included four railroad companies: surely a violation.

Secondly, section 4 provided for the creation of a sinking fund which "shall consist of the net annual income of the public works, from time to time owned by the State. . . . No part of the said sinking fund shall be used or applied otherwise than in extinguishment of the public debt, until the amount of such debt is reduced below the sum of five millions of dollars." The violation here lay in the fact that the sinking fund money was not being used to decrease the public debt, but was being given instead to private corporations.

The veto was widely approved by Pennsylvania newspapers. Many of them called it the "Railroad Swindle Bill."

The subject of railroads was again brought to the Governor, and to the entire nation, by a great strike that occurred in the anthracite region during the winter of 1871. For some time the miners in the hard coal districts had been shamefully underpaid, but so long as they were able to keep body and soul together by aid of the meager pittance allowed for labor they continued to work. Then, early in 1871, the miners received another drastic cut in wages, almost fifty per cent for certain kinds of work. From being paid $1.20 per car of coal in 1870, the diggers were reduced in 1871 to eighty-six cents a car. Since a great number of miners were paid by the car, this sharp reduction worked a real hardship. The wages paid to day laborers, or "company men," were decreased approximately thirty-five per cent. The employees rebelled at this last reduction, and under the leadership of the Workingmen's Benevolent Association, a laborer's society organized in 1860, they struck for higher pay. Since no agreement could be reached between miners and operators, the situation, going from bad to worse, culminated in a fierce three days' riot at Scranton. The conflict occurred when the striking miners refused to allow hired strike-breakers to work in their places. After many had been killed and hundreds injured, Geary, in response to various importunate demands from Scranton officials, sent Major General E. S. Osborne to the scene of trouble with a force of state militia. The presence of the troops brought a halt to the rioting and restored a precarious peace. They remained until May 25, 1871.

While the riot was at its height, President Gowen of the Reading Railroad Company conversed with the miners' representatives. Nothing of value was obtained from this conference. Gowen promised the strikers $2.50 for a ten-hour day, but the miners would not agree. They wanted $3.00 per day. A Senate investigating committee was also unable to offer any remedy to ease the tension.

The coal operators in their refusal to maintain the old level of wages protested that to do so would involve their own ruin. They would be in a position to pay more to labor if the railroads

would decrease their exorbitant freight rates. In order to keep
the price of coal from reaching prohibitive levels it was necessary to reduce the cost of production. As a result they struck
at their employees' wages.

Geary, in considering the situation, also criticized the rail-
roads for their excessive carrying charges. The particular roads
at fault were the Philadelphia and Reading; the Delaware,
Lackawanna and Western; the Lehigh and Susquehanna; the
Lehigh Valley; the Lackawanna and Bloomsburg; and the Dela-
ware and Hudson Canal Company. In order to determine their
right to charge six cents per ton per mile, the Governor asked
Attorney-General F. Carroll Brewster (who had displaced
Benjamin Brewster, a half-brother, on the latter's dismissal by
Geary) to examine the matter of high freight rates and present
a written view as to their legality. This request was made in
February, one month after the strike had started. Part of
Brewster's opinion, dated February 25, 1871, reads as follows:

I am of opinion, that as to all companies incorporated after
the adoption of the Constitution of 1857, the remedy for any
injury to the public is entirely in the hands of the Legislature.

The right of railroad and transportation companies to impose
rates of freight is a franchise, the extent of which should always
be carefully limited in the charter conferring the privilege. A
sample of the manner in which the charters of these companies
profess to protect the public interests, is to be found in an act of
incorporation, approved April 4, 1833. The restriction there used
is in these words: "The toll on any species of property shall not
exceed an average of four cents per ton per mile."

These words received a judicial construction in the case of
Boyle vs. Railroad Company, wherein it was ruled that the com-
pany "might charge for transportation in addition to the toll."
Judge Strong, in a learned opinion, examines the whole subject.
He says:

"The Legislature must be considered as having used words in
the ordinary signification, and especially so, when their technical
sense and their ordinary signification are the same. The legal
meaning of the word 'toll' is, and always has been, well defined.
It is a 'tribute or custom paid for passage,' not for carriage

—always something taken for a liberty or privilege, not for a service; and such is the common understanding of the word. Nobody supposes that tolls taken by a turnpike or canal company, include charges for transportation, or that they are anything more than an excise demanded and paid for the privilege of using the way."

Believing, as did Brewster, that legislative action should be taken on the subject, Geary referred it to the Senate. But if the Governor expected that body to rectify matters, he was bitterly disillusioned. After several sessions on the problem the Senate Judiciary Committee reported that the railroad companies had not violated their charters in raising rates to the point objected to by Geary.

Referring again to the actual strike, which is incidental to the main theme but none the less important, we find that it was eventually concluded by means of arbitration; one of the first instances, it is said, where this method was used for the settlement of disputes with the laboring classes.

In 1872 the Chief Executive had another tilt with the railroads. This time he became involved in a tax evasion issue with the famous, or infamous, Credit Mobilier Company. The very mention of this company brings to mind one of the sorriest legislative scandals ever to blacken the pages of American history. The story of the Union Pacific Railroad and the Credit Mobilier began in the grand style of American development. It ended in a congressional investigation, in disgrace and humiliation.

For years men of adventurous imagination had dreamed of linking the eastern and western shores of the United States together with iron rails. And it was in response to an ever increasing clamor that Congress, by statutory enactment in 1862 and again in 1864, authorized the building of the Union Pacific Railroad. To facilitate construction Congress gave the railroad company a right of way, a loan of twenty-seven million dollars in government bonds, and a vast stretch of the public domain. In addition the company was permitted to issue twenty-seven millions of its own first mortgage securities.

The officials of the Union Pacific then organized a construction company by purchasing the Pennsylvania Fiscal Agency, a moribund concern which had been chartered by the Pennsylvania Legislature. The company was then renamed the Credit Mobilier, the stockholders of which were practically identical with those in the Union Pacific. This inner construction ring, headed by the shrewd Oakes Ames, was in position to realize a tremendous profit through government bonds, lands, and other privileges lavished upon the Union Pacific by a prodigal Congress. It is difficult to say just how great the profits were. Ames once declared that they might total ten million dollars, but the Wilson and Hoar Committee, one of the three noted congressional groups investigating the Credit Mobilier, was certain that the inner circle reaped a sum in excess of twenty-three million dollars.

Rumors of the financial manipulations surrounding the Union Pacific began to circulate in Washington cloak rooms and lounges, and it was not long before inquisitive Representatives experienced doubt as to the ethics of the proceedings. How was all this money being made? Were such profits intended by the original statutes which provided for the railroad's contsruction? On December 9, 1867, C. C. Washburn, member of Congress from Wisconsin, introduced a bill to regulate rates on the Pacific road, and later other bills came up that worried the financiers.

Apprehensive of legislative interference, and knowing that the Credit Mobilier's activities could not stand a congressional investigation, Oakes Ames, Representative from Massachusetts, tried to quiet the fears of his financial associates by distributing shares of Credit Mobilier stock to members of Congress. These stocks were judiciously placed where Ames thought they would be most effective. The stocks, then worth 200, were sold at par, and the senators and representatives who could not immediately pay for their shares found Ames quite willing to wait until they could be paid for with accumulated dividends.

These stock transactions did not come to light until September 4, 1872, when the New York *Sun* published a startling article entitled "The King of Frauds—How the Credit Mobilier Bought Its Way Into Congress." The *Sun* charged that Oakes Ames had bribed fifteen members of Congress by distributing among them thirty thousand shares of Credit Mobilier stock valued at nine million dollars. These figures, both as to the number of congressmen involved and the shares of stock distributed among them, were greatly exaggerated.

Congress was now galvanized into action; such a revelation, extravagant or not, could not be ignored. In December 1872 James G. Blaine, Speaker of the House, called S. S. Cox to the chair and moved for the appointment of a committee to investigate charges of corruption against certain congressmen. Cox appointed George W. McCrary of Iowa, William E. Niblack of Indiana, William M. Merrick of Maryland, and Luke P. Poland of Vermont, chairman.

In short order the committee began its investigation. As the testimony proceeded a number of political figures, prominent and otherwise, found themselves affected: Vice President Colfax, John A. Logan, Roscoe Conkling, James G. Blaine, Henry L. Dawes, Henry Wilson, George S. Boutwell, John A. Bingham, James A. Garfield, William D. Kelley, James F. Wilson, James Brooks, William B. Allison, James W. Patterson, B. M. Boyer, Glenni W. Scofield, James A. Bayard, and Oakes Ames. As nothing was found against Bayard, Boutwell, Conkling, and Blaine, they were eliminated from further investigation. The others were questioned at greater length, but when the examination was completed the committee absolved all the representatives from corrupt motives except Ames and Brooks. It was the committee's recommendation that these two men be expelled from the House for bribery and corruption. But when the matter came to a vote, the House limited itself to a vote of censure against the offending members.

A committee in the Senate found Senator James Patterson of New Hampshire guilty of perjury and corruption and resolved that he be expelled. However, since his term was about to expire, no action was taken on the resolution.

That the whole unsavory business was unfortunate cannot be gainsaid. The highest legislative body in the land was made the object of nationwide suspicion, and many men who had been subjected to investigation found their future political careers embarrassed by lingering allegations of dishonesty.

The preceding review of the national aspects of the Credit Mobilier has been presented because the company affected Pennsylvania history in that it was created by that state's Legislature, also because it came into conflict with Geary over the payment of state taxes. Then, too, a comprehension of the specific is always aided materially by a review of the whole. The best review of this tax controversy is found in the Governor's annual message of 1872:

By the fourth section of the act approved May first, 1868, taxing corporations, it is declared:

"That the capital stock of all companies whatever, incorporated by or under any law of this Commonwealth . . . shall be subject to pay a tax into the Treasury of the Commonwealth annually, at the rate of one-half mill for each one per cent. of dividend made or declared by such company." The taxes received during the last four years from corporation stocks have annually exceeded one million dollars, and are now about one-sixth part of the revenue of the State.

"The Credit Mobilier of America" is a corporation created by the Legislature of Pennsylvania; and under the vast powers conferred by its charter, it undertook the construction of that great national work, the Union Pacific railroad. The first contract was made with a Mr. Hoxie for two hundred and forty-seven miles, at the eastern terminus of the road, and east of the one-hundredth meridian, for the consideration of fifty thousand dollars per mile. The contract was assigned by Hoxie to the Credit Mobilier, and the road was built by that company. In the execution of the contract certain profits were made and dividends divided by the corporation; and the taxes due thereon to the State of Pennsylvania were voluntarily paid into the Treasury. Soon afterwards another contract was made with Mr. Oakes Ames, for the construction of six hundred and sixty miles of road west of the one-hundredth meridian, for an aggregate consideration of forty-seven million nine hundred and fifteen thousand dollars. This part of the road was constructed under the latter contract; and out of the profits arising therefrom about the sum of nine million dollars was declared as dividends, and paid to the stockholders of the Credit Mobilier. But when the State demanded her taxes on these immense profits, payment was refused by the corporation, on the grounds that the dividends though paid to, and received by, the stockholders of the corporation, and in the precise amounts and proportions in which they severally held stock in the company, were yet paid to them as individuals, and not as stockholders. To make good this defence sundry papers, agreements and contracts were produced, and especially a tripartite agreement between Oakes Ames of the first part, sundry trustees therein appointed of the second part, and the Credit Mobilier of the third part, by which, and the accompanying parol evidence, it was contended the corporation was not responsible for the taxes claimed, amounting to about one million dollars. The accounting officers of the State, with counsel employed by the Auditor-General, associated with the Attorney-General, prosecuted the claim with zeal and ability, and on the two separate trials in the court of common pleas of Dauphin county recovered verdicts and judgments against the corporation.

The first was obtained November 25, 1869, for $407,483.39, and the second, December 23, 1870, for $4,610,391.03. The defendent took writs of error; and the Supreme Court reversed the judgments, and in the opinion of a majority of the judges certain principles are declared which are considered fatal to a recovery by the State. If this corporation, created by the laws of Pennsylvania, by the legerdemain of a tripartite agreement, and other contracts and proceedings to which the Commonwealth was not a party, can thus evade taxation upon its capital stock, I can imagine no good reason why every other corporation may not, by a resort to the same ingenious contrivance, escape the payment of taxation on their capital stock, and thus over a million dollars annually be lost to the State Treasury. In view of this impending danger, I earnestly invoke your prompt and careful consideration of this whole subject, and recommend such action as will in the future effectually protect the interests of the Commonwealth.

Geary's remarks have been quoted in full because they summarize briefly and clearly the entire quarrel. Also, his comments were deemed important enough to be placed in Martin and Shenk's volume, *Pennsylvania History told by Contemporaries* (previously cited), as a notable review of the state's taxing power in relation to large corporations.

The Governor's review of the matter indicates that he was considerably annoyed at the Supreme Court's decision in favor of the defendant, the Credit Mobilier Company.

The chief argument used by the lawyers of the Credit Mobilier was based on the fact that the corporation did not own the contract from which profit had been gained, and was therefore exempt from any tax claim. This claim was sustained by the Supreme Court when it handed down a decision in the following language:

"The proof arising from a settlement for taxes on dividends made by trustees under a deed of trust for stockholders of a corporation when made from the books of the trustees, is answered by showing that the corporation did not own the contract out of which the divided profits arose and which had been transferred to the trustees, but that the business had been arranged with the intention to use the corporation to conduct it, and this being prevented, it was given to the trustees to conduct for the benefit of the same persons as would have been entitled as stockholders if the corporation had undertaken the business and become the contractor, and the trustees were required to divide the profits among the stockholders of the company.

"The stockholders, instead of shielding themselves from personal liability by vesting the contract in the corporation, having personally undertaken to do the work, the Commonwealth has no claim for taxes on the profits."

The Supreme Court was unanimous in its decision (to issue a writ of error to the Dauphin County Court of Common Pleas) with the exception of Justice Daniel Agnew, who was at a loss to understand why his associates voted as they did. In a legal opinion he said:

With great respect for the judgment of my brethren, I cannot but regard this case as a departure from the landmarks of the constitutional right of trial by jury. I am not able to conceive how a fact, which has sufficient evidence to compel its submission to the jury, can be so controlled by the rebutting evidence as to require the judge to instruct the jury that they *must* find for the defendant. A judge may give his opinion upon the fact, but he must at the same time inform them it is not binding upon them as the constitutional triers of the fact.

Nine witnesses had disproved the corporation's right of ownership to the profits, but nearly all of them were stockholders in the company. Therefore, Agnew held, their credibility should have been passed upon by the Court. Since this was not done, the dissenting Justice opined that "The only remedy . . . for a verdict against the weight of evidence is a new trial, not a writ of error." He further declared that "when a judge, on a question of fact, carried to the jury by force of the evidence, can dictate the verdict, the trial by jury becomes a mere name."

Turning from the subject of railroads, let us now fix our attention on the various events which occurred during Geary's last administration concerning the revision of Pennsylvania's constitution. The weaknesses of this document, last revised in 1838, had long provoked general discussion, with continuous demands for improvement. Geary, cognizant of the public wish, presented his ideas on the matter in the annual message of January 4, 1871. Stating that four years' experience as governor had convinced him that revision was necessary, he outlined some outstanding reasons and suggestions how and why a remedy should be effected. Cited in the order of presentation they are as follows:

First. "Different systems of laws for roads, bridges, schools, elections, poor-houses and many other things, are enacted by the several counties, townships and boroughs, on subjects which ought to be regulated by general laws, operating uniformly upon all."

Second. "It is impossible for the citizens, judges of the courts, or members of the legal profession, to acquire or retain an accurate knowledge of the varying systems of laws in their respective districts: and frequently on removal from one county to another, our people find themselves under almost entirely different codes."

Third. The Governor deplored the legislative practice of making local enactments. The minds of the legislators were "so wholly absorbed by private and local bills that it is almost impossible to get a general or public act considered or passed. . . . By what is called courtesy, it is considered a breach of etiquette for any member of the Senate or House to interfere with or oppose a merely private or local bill of any other member.

"The evil could be eradicated by nothing short of 'constitutional prohibition.' "

Fourth. Special legislation was another evil that should be abolished. Further, "every bill presented for adoption should be read, at least once in full, and the yeas and nays be recorded on its final passage."

Fifth. The State Constitution should conform to the Constitution of the United States.

Sixth. The subject of minority representation should receive earnest consideration by the constitution makers.

Seventh. "The members of the General Assembly should be increased in number."

Eighth. The powers of corporations should be limited.

Ninth. "There is absolute necessity for greater security for the public funds and for their proper distribution."

Tenth. "The State Treasurer, Superintendent of Common Schools, and a Lieutenant Governor, the latter to preside over the Senate, and perform the duties of Governor, in case of his absence, sickness or death should be elected by the people."

Eleventh. "The day for holding the annual elections could, with great propriety, be changed from the Second Tuesday in October to the same day in November on which nearly all the surrounding States hold theirs."

The Governor concluded his suggestions by recommending "the Legislature to make provision for a convention to thoroughly revise and amend the Constitution of the State."

In compliance with Geary's request, the General Assembly, on June 2, 1871, passed a resolution to submit the calling of a convention to the citizens of Pennsylvania. In the general election held in October following, the people approved of the convention by a vote of 316,697 to 69,715. Another legislative Act, that of April 11, 1872, made arrangements for the calling of the convention, and, to guarantee everyone a free expression of opinion, provision was made for minority representation. One hundred and thirty-three members, the number fixed by the Legislature, met in the House of Representatives at Harrisburg on November 12, 1872. Then, fifteen days later, it adjourned to reconvene in Philadelphia on January 7, 1873, where the remainder of the sessions were held.

William M. Meredith was elected president of the Convention, but after he died, on August 17, 1873, John H. Walker, who had been serving as president *pro tempore*, was chosen to take his place. The convention concluded its labors on November 3, 1873, and on December 16 the new Constitution was submitted to the people and adopted by a vote of 253,744 to 108,594. It went into effect on January 1, 1874.

The document of 1874, still in effect but under heavy fire, made the following governmental reforms.

An increase of the number of senators and representatives of the General Assembly; biennial sessions of the Legislature; the election by the people of sundry officers heretofore chosen; minority representation; modifications of the pardoning power; a change in the tenure and mode of choosing the judiciary; a change in the date of the annual elections; prohibition of all special legislation, with other changes of vital importance to the interests of the people at large.

A lengthy review or exhaustive analysis of the Constitution
of 1873 is hardly pertinent to the main object of this book. However, suffice it to say that the instrument is still in effect, although severely criticized by many who contend that it is
archaic and inapplicable to the demands of present-day government.

Geary's second term expired on January 21, 1873, with the
inauguration of John Frederick Hartranft, the new chief executive. With justifiable cause the retiring Governor could look
back over his six years' administration and view with satisfaction
the many notable accomplishments and evidences of progress.
A review of these and a general summary of his administration
are now in order.

Geary's two administrations, reflecting the general trend of
the times, were marked by universal prosperity and well-being.
Pennsylvania's wealth from 1867 to 1873 increased greatly.
Trade and mining grew in remarkable fashion, while manufacturing, nourished by kindly protective tariffs, expanded at
a phenomenal rate of speed.

Yet all this free circulation of wealth was not an unmixed
good. It caused a "reign of shoddy" that was crudely, blatantly
extravagant. Dunaway paints a graphic picture of the era. In
his volume, *A History of Pennsylvania*, he writes:

The seamy side of all this prosperity is seen in the demoraliz-
ing effects which the Civil War and its aftermath had upon the
moral, social, and political standards of the time. It was a period
of wild extravagance on the part of the new-rich who had
acquired fortunes by profiteering during the war and by speculation in the feverish expansion that followed. Many who had
hitherto lived on scanty incomes, finding themselves suddenly
rich, set a fast pace of ostentatious display unrelieved by in-
herited standards of good taste. The effects of the war were
felt in politics also, particularly in Philadelphia, where political
corruption so abounded that it was either taken for granted or
condoned. In the maelstrom of the reconstruction period, the
ideals of the Civil War era perished and political morality sank
to new levels of degradation.

Realizing at the beginning that the state, as well as the country at large, was riding a huge financial crest, the Governor took every opportunity to reduce the public debt. On December 11, 1866, it was $37,704,409.77. When Geary's term ended this figure was reduced to $26,711,747.23. While maintaining a high quality of thriftiness, the administration was nevertheless characterized by a program which, although expensive, aimed at the alleviation of the indigent and unfortunate, particularly those who had suffered during the recent war. Seventeen million dollars went to the aid of "various institutions for the support of the deaf, dumb, blind, insane, feeble-minded, friendless, wanderers, orphans, soldiers' homes, hospitals, universities, houses of correction, penitentiaries, and the payment of military expenses . . ."

In spite of rather heavy expenditures, the trend of legislation was decidedly in favor of reduced taxation. An Act of February 23, 1866, exempted all real estate in the commonwealth from taxation for state purposes. Another Act, that of April 29, 1867, "repealed all laws requiring payment of taxes to the State on sales of loans and stocks by auctioneers." The two per cent tax on salaries, trades, occupations, offices, and professions, imposed in 1844, was removed by legislative action on April 3, 1872. In his last annual message Geary further championed the tax-reduction cause by asking the Legislature to reduce the burden imposed on manufacturing industries. In order to meet the ever increasing competition of other states, Pennsylvania, he declared, must encourage industry by liberalizing her tax laws. He feared that manufacturers would locate elsewhere unless prompt action were taken.

Geary's request that industry be relieved of certain taxes was typical of his ideas. Industry should be fostered and protected, for it was the basis of prosperity. And, responding to kind treatment, the object of gubernatorial favor throve mightily. The year 1872 saw Pennsylvania second among the states in manufactures, sixth in the production of wheat, and first in mineral wealth and resources. In 1870 the anthracite coal region produced over nineteen million tons, while the total output of bituminous coal was more than fourteen million tons.

Capitalists were further encouraged to consider Pennsylvania as a likely place to locate by the organization of a Bureau of Labor Statistics and Agriculture, which had as one of its duties the collection and dissemination of industrial and agricultural facts. As the result of the prevailing high prices farming also flourished. Acreage was increased and advances made in scientific agricultural education. Conditions were good everywhere throughout the commonwealth.

Always a friend of education, Geary devoted much time and effort to the development of Pennsylvania schools, and throughout his two administrations the school system flourished. Over forty-two million dollars were expended for the advancement of public education. Legislative appropriations amounted to approximately six hundred thousand dollars annually, while the remainder was furnished by local taxation. From 1867 to 1870 the number of school districts increased from 1,889 to 2,002; the number of schools from 13,435 to 14,212, and the number of teachers from 16,523 to 17,612. In every annual message Geary made recommendations for the improvement of Pennsylvania's educational facilities. Outstanding among them were: uniform textbooks, education for the children in alms- and poor-houses, increased pay for teachers (in 1869 the average yearly salary for teachers was $195.17), and, finally, compulsory attendance laws.

In discharging the social obligations of his high office Geary was ably assisted by his attractive second wife, formerly Mrs. Mary C. Henderson, whom he had married in November 1858. Their official receptions were gay and well managed, but any exuberance of spirit on the part of the guests came from the heart, not from the punch bowl, for Geary was a total abstainer.

He had been out of the governor's chair only a few days when the country was shocked to hear of his sudden death. On Saturday morning, February 8, 1873, while in the act of preparing some food for his infant son at the breakfast table, Geary suddenly slumped forward. When Mrs. Geary reached his side her husband was dead. The heart had failed.

The ex-Governor was placed in state in the House of Representatives on February 12, and on the following day he was buried in the Harrisburg cemetery.

Geary died in his fifty-fourth year, but although his life was brief in years, it had been full of experience and activity.

John White Geary was truly a national figure, his activities carrying him from the East to the far and middle West, and in each sphere of service his compelling personality and leadership helped to shape the course of events. Infant California, as she struggled for integration and recognition, knew his calm judgment. Through his firm and sincerely impartial gubernatorial efforts in "bleeding Kansas" that territory became less bloody, and the tragic strife which was bringing to a dangerous mental state a nation already overwrought was alleviated by his strong administration. As a lieutenant colonel he fought with great credit in the Mexican War, and fifteen years later, as a major general, he struggled against the Confederates to keep the Union intact. Geary concluded a brilliant career by serving two terms as Governor of Pennsylvania, where he added to an already admirable record by heading an administration which was noted for its progressiveness and efficiency. Thoroughly masculine, and a fighter to his finger tips, Geary takes his place beside the finest Americans of the nineteenth century.

BIBLIOGRAPHICAL NOTE

MANUSCRIPTS

A. *Official*

The Kansas Territorial Papers, May 30, 1854, to June 27, 1858, in the Department of State, Washington, D.C., were disappointingly meager in the amount of material relating directly to Geary, but they are important for a study of the Kansas troubles. Likewise applicable to the quarrel in Kansas is a collection of Miscellaneous Letters also in the Department of State. They too provided little of material aid on Geary's activities in Kansas.

B. *Unofficial*

Undoubtedly the most important source on Geary's service in the Mexican War is to be found in his Diary which covers all his war adventures up to the signing of the treaty of Guadalupe Hidalgo. It is in the possession of his grandson, Alfred H. Geary, who resides in Rosemont, Pa. Also in Mr. Geary's collection are some letters and papers relating to his grandfather, but they are lamentably few in number. The Papers of Simon Cameron in the Manuscript Division of the Library of Congress were consulted for information relating to Cameron's sponsorship of Geary in the Pennsylvania gubernatorial contest of 1866. Unfortunately they throw little new light on the election, one letter only proving of value. The Pierce Collection of letters, also located in the Library of Congress, provides valuable information on Geary's short executive career in Kansas. The circumstances surrounding his return to political life after the Civil War may be found in the John Covode Papers on deposit at the Historical Society of Western Pennsylvania, in Pittsburgh. Six letters of a general nature, written by and relating to Geary, can be found at the Historical Society of Pennsylvania, in Philadelphia. Especially interesting is one written by Geary to James Buchanan.

A. *Official Documents*

Of course in a study of this nature it is impossible to omit the *Kansas Historical Collections*, 1889–96 (Topeka, 1896). Volumes IV and V contain extremely valuable information on the Kansas troubles and on Geary's part in them. Without the Executive Minutes and Letters herein contained the chapter on Kansas would have been brief indeed. Any student engaged in the study of the life of a Pennsylvania governor of this period cannot ignore the speeches and reports in the *Pennsylvania Archives*, Fourth Series (twelve volumes, Harrisburg, 1902). Volumes VIII and IX were valuable for Geary's two administrations. This is equally true of the *Pennsylvania State Reports*, Volume XVII, edited by P. Frazer Smith (Philadelphia, 1872).

B. *Unofficial Collection*

Asa Earl Martin and Hiram Herr Shenk in their book entitled *Pennsylvania History Told by Contemporaries* (New York, 1925), have arranged in chronological order a series of papers which they deem of importance in the growth of Pennsylvania. The volume is subject to the limitations of such collections, but on the whole the documents contained therein have been judiciously selected as well as helpfully described in short prefatory notes at the head of each source.

C. *Newspapers*

Of tremendous aid was a collection of nineteen scrapbooks composed almost entirely of newspaper clippings relating, for the most part, directly to Geary. A great many of the newspaper references used in this volume were obtained from this valuable collection. For a study of Pennsylvania politics from 1865 to 1873 these scrapbooks, totaling approximately three thousand pages, would be well-nigh indispensable. They may be found at the residence of Alfred H. Geary, Rosemont, Pa. In all, twenty-one newspapers, or clippings therefrom, were used in this study. Of most value was the Philadelphia *Public Ledger*.

D. *Printed Contemporary Works*

Although biased and highly laudatory, John H. Gihon's *Geary and Kansas* (Philadelphia, 1857) is important for Geary's administration in Kansas during 1856. Gihon was in Kansas at the time, acting as private secretary to Geary. Fortunately he does not hesitate to include several pertinent letters and papers, many of which are to be found in the *Kansas Historical Collections* cited above. Frank Soule, John H. Gihon, and James Nesbit in their volume *The Annals of San Francisco* (New York, 1854), present a fairly accurate account of the hectic early days of San Francisco. It contains a biographical sketch of Geary and an account of his term as mayor.

SECONDARY SOURCE IN MANUSCRIPT

One of the most unusual discoveries made in connection with the present research was an unpublished work entitled "Life and Public Services of John White Geary," now possessed by Alfred H. Geary. Highly verbose, careless, melodramatic, and above all inaccurate, the author, who remains unidentified, lauds his hero beyond all the limits of propriety. Any facts gleaned from this unique work had to be handled with particular caution and checked against more trustworthy sources, for its occasional inaccuracies rendered it extremely unreliable. The first two chapters, presumably dealing with Geary's early life, are missing.

SECONDARY SOURCES

For any study of the Mexican War one work is always found to be of absolute indispensability. This is Justin H. Smith's *The War With Mexico* (two volumes, New York, 1919). Undoubtedly Smith's effort still remains the best contribution to the history of that conflict. Also quite helpful was J. F. H. Claiborne's *Life and Correspondence of John A. Quitman* (two volumes, New York, 1860).

A very readable account of American expansion into California can be found in a volume by Rockwell D. Hunt and Nellie

Van De Grift Sanchez, *A Short History of California* (New York, 1929). Romantic and rather appealing in style is Stewart Edward White's *The Forty Niners* (New Haven, 1921).

For the Kansas imbroglio Charles Robinson's *The Kansas Conflict* (New York, 1892) is of value although strongly biased in favor of the free-soil settlers. Entertainingly written but not at all definitive is Leverett Wilson Spring's *Kansas* (New York, 1885). As a general account J. N. Holloway's *History of Kansas* (Lafayette, 1868) is hardly adequate. He handles the turbulent period of Kansas history with an illusory naïveté that leaves much to be desired. For a penetrating discussion on James Buchanan's betrayal of Robert J. Walker, Geary's successor as governor of the territory, see George D. Harmon, *Aspects of Slavery and Expansion, 1848-60* (Bethlehem, 1929).

In an appraisal of some of the works consulted for material on the Civil War it must be noted that Volume II of Samuel P. Bates's praiseworthy *History of Pennsylvania Volunteers* (five volumes, Harrisburg, 1869) furnished indispensable information on Geary's Civil War service with the Twenty-eighth Pennsylvania Volunteers. Of equal importance is his *Martial Deeds of Pennsylvania* (Philadelphia, 1876). Although occasional reference only is made to Geary in the following books on the Civil War they nevertheless provide much necessary background material on the campaigns in which he participated. They are: R. V. Johnson and C. C. Buel, editors, *Battles and Leaders of the Civil War*, Volume III (four volumes, New York, 1887-88); John Bigelow, *The Campaign of Chancellorsville* (New Haven, 1910); S. M. Bowman and R. B. Irwin, *Sherman and His Campaigns* (New York, 1865); Henry M. Cist, *The Army of the Cumberland* (New York, 1882).

For general Pennsylvania history the best book yet written is Wayland Fuller Dunaway's *A History of Pennsylvania* (New York, 1935). With so fine a command of the subject it is to be regretted that Professor Dunaway did not produce a work of greater length. Contained in William C. Armor's *Lives of the Governors of Pennsylvania* (Philadelphia, 1872) is a brief but dependable sketch of Geary's career. It provided the best account of Geary's early life. Invaluable for a study of Pennsylvania politics from 1838 to 1905 is A. K. McClure's *Old Time*

Notes of Pennsylvania (two volumes, Philadelphia, 1905). Involved in many campaigns, Mr. McClure presents inside political information that is hard to duplicate elsewhere. For references on Geary's administrations Volume II is of considerable aid. Of little value for a study of this nature were William H. Egle's *An Illustrated History of the Commonwealth of Pennsylvania* (Harrisburg, 1876) and L. S. Shimmel's *A History of Pennsylvania* (New York, 1900).

INDEX